Table of Contents

Introduction 7

The Emergence of Bitcoin: Explore the revolutionary advent of Bitcoin and its impact on the financial landscape. 7

The Promise of Decentralization: Understand the vision of decentralization and how it shaped the early crypto world. 11

The Lack of Regulation: Analyze the absence of regulatory frameworks and oversight that exposed the crypto space to vulnerabilities. 15

Chapter 1: The First Altcoins 19

Altcoin Pioneers: Discover the early altcoins that aimed to challenge Bitcoin's dominance. 19

Vulnerabilities Explored: Investigate the security flaws in early altcoin projects that made them susceptible to rugpulls. 24

Impact on Investors: Examine how rugpulls affected investors' confidence and the perception of altcoins. 29

Chapter 2: Decentralized Finance Experiments 33

The Birth of DeFi: Unravel the pioneering experiments of decentralized finance and its potential to disrupt traditional finance. 33

Smart Contract Vulnerabilities: Explore the technical vulnerabilities within DeFi smart contracts that led to rugpulls. *38*

Lessons in Code and Trust: Understand the importance of robust coding and trustless systems in DeFi projects. *43*

Chapter 3: The Great ICO Gold Rush 48

ICO Frenzy: Dive into the Initial Coin Offering (ICO) mania and the promise of easy fundraising for crypto projects. .. *48*

The Rise of Scams: Expose the deceptive ICO projects that exploited investors' excitement and trust. *53*

Regulatory Vacuum: Discuss the lack of regulatory guidance and how it contributed to the proliferation of scams. *58*

Chapter 4: Hacking and Exploits 63

The Dark Side of Crypto: Investigate high-profile hacks and exploits that targeted early crypto exchanges and projects *63*

Security Breaches: Analyze the weak points in exchange platforms and project infrastructures that were exploited. *68*

Repercussions on Trust: Examine how hacking incidents affected investor trust in the safety of the crypto space. *73*

Chapter 5: Social Engineering and Manipulation .. 77

Copyright © 2023 by Ethan J. Monroe (Author)

All rights reserved. No part of this book may be reproduced or utilized in any form or by any means, electronic or mechanical, including photocopying, recording or by any information storage and retrieval system, without permission in writing from the publisher, except for brief quotations in critical articles or reviews.

The content of this book is based on various sources and is intended for educational and entertainment purposes only. While the author has made every effort to ensure the accuracy, completeness, and reliability of the information provided, the information may be subject to errors, omissions, or inaccuracies. Therefore, the author makes no warranties, express or implied, regarding the content of this book.

Readers are advised to seek the guidance of a licensed professional before attempting any techniques or actions outlined in this book. The author is not responsible for any losses, damages, or injuries that may arise from the use of information contained within. The information provided in this book is not intended to be a substitute for professional advice, and readers should not rely solely on the information presented.

By reading this book, readers acknowledge that the author is not providing legal, financial, medical, or professional advice. Any reliance on the information contained in this book is solely at the reader's own risk.

Thank you for selecting this book as a valuable source of knowledge and inspiration. Our aim is to provide you with insights and information that will enrich your understanding and enhance your personal growth. We appreciate your decision to embark on this journey of discovery with us, and we hope that this book will exceed your expectations and leave a lasting impact on your life.

Title: Rugpulls Genesis: Birth of Crypto's Vulnerabilities
Subtitle: Altcoin Pioneers: The Rise of Bitcoin's Competitors

Series: Rugpulls Unveiled: Untangling the Web of Deceit in Early Crypto
Author: Ethan J. Monroe

Psychological Tactics: Uncover the methods used by scammers to manipulate public perception and promote fraudulent projects. 77

FOMO and FUD: Explore how Fear Of Missing Out (FOMO) and Fear, Uncertainty, and Doubt (FUD) were leveraged to influence the market. 81

The Human Factor: Discuss the role of social engineering and human vulnerabilities in facilitating rugpulls. 86

Chapter 6: Learning from Mistakes 91

Community Responses: Witness how the crypto community rallied to expose and learn from rugpull incidents. 91

Improved Due Diligence: Understand how investors and projects began adopting better due diligence practices. 95

Building Resilience: Explore the steps taken to fortify the crypto ecosystem against future rugpulls. 99

Chapter 7: Regulation on the Horizon 103

The Call for Regulation: Delve into the debates surrounding the need for regulatory oversight in the crypto world. 103

Early Efforts: Examine the first attempts at implementing regulatory measures to curb rugpulls. 108

Striking the Balance: Discuss the challenges of regulating a decentralized and global industry. 112

Conclusion 116

The Evolution of Crypto: Reflect on how the early years shaped the trajectory of the crypto space. 116
Lessons for the Future: Summarize the key takeaways and cautionary lessons from the era of rugpulls. 121
The Road Ahead: Look forward to a more resilient and secure future for cryptocurrencies and decentralized finance. 126
Wordbook **131**
Supplementary Materials **135**

Introduction

The Emergence of Bitcoin: Explore the revolutionary advent of Bitcoin and its impact on the financial landscape.

The world was on the cusp of a digital revolution when a mysterious whitepaper, titled "Bitcoin: A Peer-to-Peer Electronic Cash System," was published in 2008 under the pseudonym Satoshi Nakamoto. Little did the world know that this whitepaper would pave the way for a groundbreaking invention that would disrupt the very foundations of finance and give birth to an entire ecosystem of cryptocurrencies.

Bitcoin's Genesis: A Digital Revolution Unfolds

The emergence of Bitcoin was not just about a new form of currency; it represented a paradigm shift in how we perceive value, trust, and financial transactions. At its core, Bitcoin is a decentralized digital currency, designed to be immune to censorship and control by any central authority. This concept, known as decentralization, was revolutionary in a world where financial systems were traditionally centralized and controlled by governments and banks.

The Seeds of Decentralization: Redefining Trust

Bitcoin's true innovation was its utilization of blockchain technology. The blockchain, a public and immutable digital ledger, was the backbone of the Bitcoin network. It offered transparency, security, and the ability to conduct transactions without intermediaries. This redefined the very concept of trust, as participants no longer needed to rely on financial institutions to facilitate transactions or validate ownership.

Impact on the Financial Landscape: A New Digital Frontier

As Bitcoin gained traction, it quickly became more than just a digital experiment. People from all walks of life began to see its potential to challenge traditional financial systems. Its limited supply of 21 million coins and decentralized nature brought economic scarcity to the digital realm, and this scarcity, in turn, generated interest and investment.

From Skepticism to Mainstream Recognition

However, Bitcoin faced its fair share of skepticism. Critics questioned its value, its legality, and its feasibility as a long-term financial instrument. But as the technology matured and the Bitcoin network proved its resilience, it garnered attention from investors, technologists, and even institutions.

Bitcoin's Ripple Effect: Inspiring an Ecosystem

The success of Bitcoin inspired the creation of thousands of other cryptocurrencies, commonly referred to as altcoins. Each of these altcoins aimed to replicate the decentralized, trustless model that Bitcoin introduced. Some sought to improve upon Bitcoin's limitations, while others introduced novel features and functionalities.

Catalyzing Financial Inclusion and Freedom

Bitcoin also had profound implications beyond its potential as an investment vehicle. In regions with limited access to traditional financial services, Bitcoin offered a gateway to participate in the global economy. Its borderless nature allowed individuals to send and receive funds across the world, bypassing traditional intermediaries and their associated fees.

The Future Beckons: Unveiling the Promise

As the first chapter of this book explores the emergence of Bitcoin, it sets the stage for understanding the vulnerabilities and challenges that plagued the cryptocurrency space. From its revolutionary inception, Bitcoin ignited a spark that would ignite a fire of innovation, experimentation, and unfortunately, exploitation. The subsequent chapters will delve into the rugpull incidents that emerged as the crypto world evolved, shedding light on the intricacies of these incidents, their impact, and the lessons learned.

As we journey through the pages of this book, we will uncover not only the vulnerabilities that existed but also the resilience and determination of the crypto community to build a more secure and trustworthy ecosystem. The story of Bitcoin's emergence is one of disruption, hope, and transformation, and it provides the backdrop against which the events of the crypto world unfolded.

The Promise of Decentralization: Understand the vision of decentralization and how it shaped the early crypto world.

In the wake of the 2008 global financial crisis, a sense of disillusionment with traditional financial systems was pervasive. People across the world were seeking alternatives that would empower individuals, reduce dependence on intermediaries, and usher in a new era of transparency and fairness. It was within this context that the concept of decentralization emerged as a beacon of hope, offering a fundamental reimagining of how financial systems and transactions could operate.

The Visionaries and the Quest for Empowerment

Decentralization wasn't an idea born overnight; it was the culmination of years of technological innovation and philosophical reflection. Bitcoin's creator, the enigmatic Satoshi Nakamoto, envisioned a world where individuals could transact directly with each other, unencumbered by the need for banks or other intermediaries. This vision was a direct response to the failures of the centralized financial systems that had led to the economic turmoil of 2008.

The Architecture of Trustlessness: Redefining Interactions

At the heart of decentralization lies the concept of trustlessness. In traditional systems, trust is vested in intermediaries – banks, governments, and financial institutions that oversee transactions. However, these institutions are not immune to errors, corruption, or self-interest. Decentralization sought to replace this blind trust with cryptographic proof and mathematical consensus mechanisms.

Blockchain: A Technological Revolution

Central to the concept of decentralization is the blockchain – an immutable and distributed ledger that records transactions transparently and securely. The blockchain not only allowed for peer-to-peer transactions but also introduced a level of transparency that was previously unthinkable. Every transaction was recorded in a way that anyone could verify, revolutionizing accountability in financial interactions.

Shaping the Early Crypto World: Beyond Currency

While Bitcoin was the first manifestation of the decentralized vision, its impact extended far beyond being a digital currency. It laid the groundwork for a new paradigm of applications built on decentralized principles. This led to the birth of the concept of "smart contracts," self-executing agreements with terms directly written into code. These contracts could automate various processes, reducing the need for intermediaries and human intervention.

Egalitarianism and Financial Inclusion

One of the most compelling promises of decentralization was its potential to foster financial inclusion on a global scale. With a smartphone and an internet connection, anyone, regardless of their geographic location or socioeconomic status, could access and participate in the decentralized ecosystem. This inclusivity had the potential to bridge gaps in traditional financial systems and provide opportunities for economic growth and empowerment.

Challenges and Controversies: Striking the Balance

While the promise of decentralization was intoxicating, it wasn't without challenges. Questions about scalability, governance, and the environmental impact of certain blockchain technologies arose. Additionally, the decentralized nature of cryptocurrencies raised concerns about their potential misuse for illicit activities. Striking a balance between the vision of decentralization and the practical realities of implementation became a focal point for the evolving crypto world.

Setting the Stage: A Prelude to Vulnerabilities

As we delve into the early chapters of this book, exploring the promise of decentralization sets the context for understanding how rugpull incidents emerged. The very principles that fueled the decentralization movement also inadvertently created vulnerabilities that bad actors sought to exploit. In the following chapters, we will examine how these vulnerabilities were exploited, the impact they had, and the lessons that have been learned as the crypto community continues to navigate the intricate landscape of decentralized finance.

 The journey through the early days of the crypto world will not only uncover the mechanics of decentralization but also the challenges that tested its viability and resilience. From the promise of empowerment to the pitfalls of unchecked innovation, the crypto story is one of aspiration, adaptation, and ultimately, maturation.

The Lack of Regulation: Analyze the absence of regulatory frameworks and oversight that exposed the crypto space to vulnerabilities.

The emergence of cryptocurrencies marked a bold step toward reshaping the financial landscape. As digital assets gained prominence, their decentralized nature brought promises of financial empowerment, privacy, and a break from traditional financial intermediaries. Yet, this very lack of centralization and regulation, while a source of innovation and freedom, also exposed the nascent crypto space to a unique set of vulnerabilities.

The Regulatory Void: Uncharted Territories

In the early days of cryptocurrencies, the regulatory landscape resembled uncharted territories. Traditional financial frameworks struggled to accommodate digital assets that operated independently of established institutions. This regulatory void gave rise to a sense of both excitement and uncertainty, as entrepreneurs and investors sought to explore the potential of this new frontier.

A Double-Edged Sword: Freedom and Risk

The absence of traditional regulatory oversight was celebrated by many as a hallmark of cryptocurrencies. It allowed for innovation to thrive without the burdens of bureaucratic red tape. However, this very freedom also laid the groundwork for exploitation and abuse, as malicious actors recognized the lack of safeguards and accountability.

The Genesis of Vulnerabilities: Initial Coin Offerings (ICOs)

One of the earliest manifestations of the regulatory gap was the Initial Coin Offering (ICO) phenomenon. ICOs provided a novel way for projects to raise funds directly from the public, bypassing traditional venture capital channels. While this democratization of fundraising was promising, it was accompanied by a wave of fraudulent and scam projects that took advantage of the lack of regulatory scrutiny.

Wild West: Crypto Exchanges and Market Manipulation

As cryptocurrencies gained traction, exchanges sprouted across the digital landscape, facilitating the trading of various tokens. These exchanges were largely unregulated, and their vulnerabilities were exploited by hackers and manipulators. Lack of proper security measures and transparency allowed for significant market manipulation, leaving traders and investors exposed to substantial risks.

Emergence of Security Breaches and Hacks

The decentralized nature of cryptocurrencies attracted not only legitimate actors but also malicious ones. High-profile security breaches and hacks plagued exchanges and projects, leading to significant financial losses. The lack of standardized security practices across the industry meant that vulnerabilities were often overlooked until exploited.

Navigating the Terrain: Challenges in Legal Classification

The unique nature of cryptocurrencies posed a conundrum for regulators attempting to classify them within existing legal frameworks. Were they currencies, commodities, securities, or something entirely new? This classification dilemma hindered the development of clear regulations and left many aspects of the crypto space in a regulatory gray area.

Rise of Regulatory Initiatives: Responses to Exploitation

As the vulnerabilities and risks became increasingly apparent, regulatory initiatives began to take shape. Governments and international bodies recognized the need to protect investors and curb illicit activities. However, the challenge of implementing effective regulations without stifling innovation remained.

The Confluence of Regulation and Decentralization

One of the most complex aspects of regulating the crypto space was the inherent clash between the decentralized ethos of cryptocurrencies and the need for oversight. Striking a balance between safeguarding investors and preserving the unique attributes of cryptocurrencies proved to be a formidable task.

From Vulnerabilities to Resilience: Lessons Learned

In navigating the regulatory landscape of cryptocurrencies, the crypto community learned invaluable lessons. The lack of oversight had exposed vulnerabilities that required addressing. Through collaboration, education, and an evolving understanding of the space, stakeholders began to work toward building a more secure and robust ecosystem.

Conclusion: A Safer Future, a Resilient Crypto Landscape

As we embark on the journey through this book, exploring the impact of rugpull incidents and vulnerabilities in the crypto space, the analysis of the lack of regulation becomes a pivotal backdrop. The absence of regulatory frameworks, while fostering innovation, allowed for vulnerabilities to surface. As we delve deeper into specific case studies and their aftermath, we'll witness the impact of this regulatory gap on the crypto community and gain insights into the measures taken to fortify the crypto landscape against future threats.

Chapter 1: The First Altcoins

Altcoin Pioneers: Discover the early altcoins that aimed to challenge Bitcoin's dominance.

As the concept of cryptocurrencies gained traction with the introduction of Bitcoin, it wasn't long before other innovative minds entered the scene, seeking to build upon the foundations laid by Bitcoin's blockchain technology. These early contenders, known as "altcoins" (short for alternative coins), emerged with the ambitious goal of challenging Bitcoin's dominance while introducing new features and addressing perceived limitations. This chapter delves into the origins of these altcoins, their motivations, and the unique contributions they brought to the evolving crypto landscape.

The Spark of Innovation: Diversification Beyond Bitcoin

Bitcoin, as the first cryptocurrency, held a place of honor as a groundbreaking invention. However, it wasn't long before visionaries and technologists recognized the potential for further innovation in the blockchain space. These pioneers sought to create alternative cryptocurrencies that could offer distinct benefits and use cases beyond what Bitcoin had initially offered.

Litecoin: Silver to Bitcoin's Gold

Among the earliest altcoins, Litecoin stood out as a notable contender. Created by Charlie Lee in 2011, Litecoin aimed to address some of the scalability issues associated with Bitcoin. Its adoption of the "Scrypt" algorithm allowed for faster transaction confirmations, making it suitable for smaller, everyday transactions.

Namecoin: Beyond Currency to Decentralized Identity

Namecoin, introduced in 2011, ventured into uncharted territory by combining cryptocurrency with domain name registration. Its blockchain served as both a decentralized currency and a system for registering and managing domain names in a censorship-resistant manner. This innovation paved the way for exploring blockchain's potential in domains beyond financial transactions.

Peercoin: Introducing Proof of Stake

In 2012, Peercoin made its debut by introducing an alternative consensus mechanism known as "Proof of Stake." While Bitcoin relied on energy-intensive Proof of Work, Peercoin introduced a more energy-efficient approach, where the amount of cryptocurrency held by participants influenced their ability to mine new blocks.

Emerging Use Cases: Nxt and Beyond

The altcoin landscape continued to expand, giving rise to projects like Nxt in 2013. Nxt introduced a platform for creating decentralized applications and smart contracts, building upon the concept of blockchain technology for more than just currency transactions. This pioneering move laid the groundwork for the later explosion of decentralized finance (DeFi) applications.

The Momentum Builds: Ripple and Dash

As the altcoin landscape matured, a few projects gained significant attention. Ripple, for instance, sought to revolutionize cross-border payments by facilitating real-time, cross-currency transactions for financial institutions. Dash, on the other hand, introduced innovations like Masternodes, which enabled advanced features like instant transactions and decentralized governance.

An Evolving Ecosystem: Ethereum's Impact

While the early altcoins paved the way for diversification and experimentation, it was Ethereum's introduction in 2015 that would truly redefine the possibilities of blockchain technology. Ethereum introduced the concept of smart contracts on a larger scale, enabling developers to build decentralized applications and entire ecosystems within its blockchain.

Altcoin Impact: Catalyst for Innovation

The emergence of altcoins highlighted the collaborative and competitive nature of the crypto landscape.

While some altcoins aimed to directly challenge Bitcoin's dominance, others focused on specific use cases, technological improvements, or even experimental concepts. This diversity sparked innovation, fostering the growth of an ecosystem that explored the full potential of blockchain technology.

Looking Forward: Altcoins as Precursors to DeFi

As the crypto space evolved, the concepts introduced by early altcoins set the stage for the explosion of decentralized finance (DeFi) applications. The experiments in alternative consensus mechanisms, innovative use cases, and scalability solutions paved the way for the complex financial instruments and protocols that would reshape the financial industry in the years to come.

Conclusion: Seeds of Diversity and Growth

The altcoin pioneers, each with their unique visions, contributed to the development of a crypto landscape that extended beyond Bitcoin's singular purpose. Their experiments and innovations laid the groundwork for the exploration of blockchain's potential in diverse industries, ultimately leading to the evolution of decentralized finance and the myriad possibilities it holds. In the subsequent chapters, we will delve into the vulnerabilities that some of these altcoins encountered and the impact of rugpull incidents on their projects and the wider crypto community.

Vulnerabilities Explored: Investigate the security flaws in early altcoin projects that made them susceptible to rugpulls.

While the early altcoins sought to expand the capabilities of blockchain technology and provide alternatives to Bitcoin, their innovative ambitions were accompanied by a range of security vulnerabilities. These vulnerabilities, often stemming from experimental features and a lack of mature development practices, rendered several early altcoin projects susceptible to rugpull incidents. In this chapter, we delve into the security flaws that emerged within these projects, examining their origins, impact, and the lessons they imparted to the evolving crypto landscape.

Early Days, Early Challenges: A Maturing Ecosystem

The altcoin pioneers operated in an environment that was still coming to terms with the intricacies of blockchain technology. Unlike Bitcoin, which had the advantage of being the first to showcase the security of blockchain, early altcoins often faced hurdles in implementing and testing their innovations. The vulnerabilities that emerged were both technical and conceptual, reflecting the uncharted territory they were navigating.

Experimental Features and Unintended Consequences

Many early altcoins introduced novel features that aimed to distinguish them from Bitcoin. However, the introduction of such features often came at the cost of rigorous testing and review. These experimental components introduced unanticipated vulnerabilities that bad actors could exploit. One notable example was Namecoin's decentralized domain registration, which, while innovative, suffered from vulnerabilities that affected the integrity of the domain name system.

Smart Contracts and Code Vulnerabilities

As altcoins explored functionalities beyond currency, some projects ventured into the realm of smart contracts. The introduction of programmable contracts within altcoin blockchains created new opportunities for innovation, but it also introduced complexities that were not fully understood. Vulnerabilities in smart contract code allowed malicious actors to exploit loopholes and execute unintended actions, leading to loss of funds and trust within these ecosystems.

Inadequate Security Measures: A Common Theme

Security practices within the early altcoin projects often lagged behind the pace of innovation. The urgency to release new features and attract users sometimes led to a neglect of security considerations. Weaknesses in network protocols, poor encryption practices, and insufficient auditing procedures left openings for attackers to infiltrate and manipulate these nascent ecosystems.

Lack of Developer Experience and External Threats

The early altcoin projects frequently faced a shortage of experienced developers familiar with the nuances of blockchain technology. This skill gap, combined with the evolving nature of the technology, created vulnerabilities that bad actors were quick to exploit. Additionally, external threats, such as Distributed Denial of Service (DDoS) attacks, posed challenges that further exposed these projects to risks.

The Rise of Pump and Dump Schemes

As altcoins gained attention and value, they attracted not only genuine investors but also those seeking to exploit the hype for personal gain. The vulnerabilities in these projects provided opportunities for "pump and dump" schemes, where malicious actors artificially inflated the value of a token through coordinated efforts, only to sell off their holdings at a profit, leaving genuine investors with significant losses.

Lessons Learned Through Vulnerability

The vulnerabilities that emerged within early altcoin projects were harsh but vital lessons for the crypto community. The importance of thorough code audits, rigorous testing, and a commitment to security became evident. The rugpull incidents illuminated the necessity for a holistic approach to development that prioritizes not only innovation but also the protection of users' assets and trust.

Evolution of Best Practices: Strengthening the Ecosystem

As the crypto landscape matured, the lessons learned from the vulnerabilities in early altcoin projects catalyzed the development of best practices. The focus shifted toward comprehensive security audits, robust testing, and the implementation of measures to prevent and mitigate attacks. These changes contributed to the ongoing evolution of the crypto ecosystem, as security-conscious development became a cornerstone of blockchain projects.

Conclusion: From Vulnerabilities to Vigilance

The vulnerabilities explored within early altcoin projects showcased the dynamic and challenging nature of building in the crypto space. They underlined the importance of balancing innovation with security and fostering an environment of continuous improvement. As we delve further into this book, analyzing the impact of rugpull incidents, these early vulnerabilities will serve as a foundation for understanding the complexities of maintaining trust and security within a decentralized and rapidly evolving ecosystem.

Impact on Investors: Examine how rugpulls affected investors' confidence and the perception of altcoins.

As early altcoins emerged, they brought with them a sense of novelty and promise. These projects aimed to challenge the dominance of Bitcoin while introducing new features and innovative use cases. However, alongside their potential benefits, they also carried vulnerabilities that some malicious actors exploited, leading to rugpull incidents. This chapter delves into the profound impact that these rugpulls had on investors' confidence and the overall perception of altcoins within the cryptocurrency ecosystem.

Initial Euphoria and Growing Hesitation

In the early days of altcoins, excitement ran high as investors saw the potential for substantial returns and the diversification of their portfolios. As projects introduced unique features and innovative technologies, they garnered attention from both early adopters and seasoned investors. However, as the frequency of rugpull incidents increased, this initial euphoria gradually gave way to a growing sense of hesitation and skepticism.

The Trust Deficit: A Fundamental Blow

Rugpull incidents, characterized by projects abandoning development or maliciously manipulating token prices, shattered the trust that investors had placed in the promise of altcoins. These incidents showcased the vulnerability of even well-intentioned projects to exploitation, leading investors to question the legitimacy of the entire altcoin ecosystem. The resulting erosion of trust had ripple effects that extended beyond individual projects.

Fear of Loss: A Lingering Concern

The rugpulls introduced a fear of financial loss among investors, making them more cautious and discerning about where they placed their funds. The notion that even established projects could succumb to vulnerabilities undermined the perception that altcoins were a reliable investment choice. Investors became more reluctant to engage with altcoins, fearing that their efforts and capital might be squandered by unscrupulous actors.

Altcoin Reputation: A Double-Edged Sword

As rugpull incidents became more prominent, the reputation of altcoins suffered a significant blow. While the intention behind altcoins was often noble, the rugpulls cast a shadow over the entire category, leading to generalizations that labeled all altcoins as high-risk and volatile. This tarnished reputation had long-term implications for legitimate projects, hindering their ability to gain trust and recognition from potential investors.

Erosion of Confidence in Developer Teams

Investors often place significant trust in the teams behind altcoin projects, expecting them to have the knowledge and commitment to navigate the complex blockchain landscape. Rugpull incidents exposed vulnerabilities in developer teams' abilities to secure and maintain their projects, leading investors to question the competency and credibility of these teams. This erosion of confidence strained the relationship between projects and their supporters.

Regulatory Scrutiny and Investor Protection

The prevalence of rugpulls prompted regulators to take notice and consider the need for investor protection within the cryptocurrency space. The lack of regulation made it challenging for investors to seek recourse or hold malicious actors accountable. Regulatory discussions often intensified in the wake of rugpull incidents, leading to debates about the necessity of oversight and its potential impact on innovation.

Emergence of Due Diligence Practices

The rugpull incidents forced investors to adopt a more cautious approach. They began to conduct thorough due diligence on projects before investing, scrutinizing whitepapers, team backgrounds, code repositories, and community engagement. While these practices were essential for investor protection, they also contributed to a more discerning and risk-averse investor landscape.

Rebuilding Trust: Community Initiatives

In response to the declining trust caused by rugpulls, the crypto community began to rally around initiatives that aimed to identify and expose potential scams. Community-driven efforts to scrutinize projects and share insights played a crucial role in rebuilding confidence. These initiatives underscored the decentralized nature of the cryptocurrency ecosystem, where collective vigilance became a defense against malicious actors.

Conclusion: Navigating the Fallout

The rugpull incidents within the early altcoin landscape had far-reaching consequences that stretched beyond individual projects. Investors faced a crisis of confidence, and the perception of altcoins as a whole suffered. The aftermath of these rugpulls highlighted the necessity for robust security practices, transparent communication, and collective efforts to protect the integrity of the altcoin ecosystem. As we proceed through this book, exploring the rugpull incidents and their implications, the impact on investors' confidence and perception will remain a critical backdrop for understanding the broader context of these events.

Chapter 2: Decentralized Finance Experiments
The Birth of DeFi: Unravel the pioneering experiments of decentralized finance and its potential to disrupt traditional finance.

The emergence of cryptocurrencies laid the foundation for a fundamental rethinking of traditional financial systems. While the initial focus was on digital currencies, the true revolution came with the exploration of how blockchain technology could reshape the entire financial landscape. This chapter delves into the birth of decentralized finance (DeFi) – a movement that aimed to disrupt traditional finance through the principles of decentralization, transparency, and permissionless innovation.

From Currency to Finance: Expanding Possibilities

In the early years of cryptocurrencies, the focus was primarily on creating alternatives to traditional currencies. Bitcoin paved the way by showcasing the potential of decentralized transactions, but the visionaries within the crypto community saw an opportunity to extend the application of blockchain technology beyond simple payments. The concept of DeFi emerged from this desire to reimagine financial services.

Smart Contracts: The Catalyst for Transformation

The introduction of smart contracts, self-executing pieces of code that automate agreements and transactions, was a turning point in the evolution of blockchain technology. Ethereum, launched in 2015, became the breeding ground for these revolutionary contracts, enabling developers to create applications that went far beyond simple transactions. Smart contracts formed the cornerstone of DeFi, allowing for the creation of complex financial instruments on a decentralized platform.

Decentralization's Promise: Disintermediation and Inclusion

Traditional financial systems are often centralized, relying on intermediaries like banks, insurers, and brokers to facilitate transactions. DeFi sought to eliminate these intermediaries, allowing users to engage directly with financial services through blockchain technology. This disintermediation not only reduced fees and processing times but also had the potential to include individuals who were previously excluded from traditional finance due to geographic or economic barriers.

The Building Blocks of DeFi: Lending, Borrowing, and More

The DeFi movement introduced a range of innovative applications, each challenging a different aspect of traditional finance. Lending and borrowing platforms enabled users to lend out their cryptocurrencies in exchange for interest or borrow assets without needing a traditional bank. Decentralized exchanges allowed users to trade assets directly with one another, avoiding the need for a central authority.

Automated Market Makers and Liquidity Pools

Automated market makers (AMMs) were a groundbreaking innovation within the DeFi ecosystem. These algorithms enabled users to provide liquidity to decentralized exchanges by contributing to liquidity pools. In return, users received a share of trading fees. This concept revolutionized liquidity provision, making it accessible to anyone with cryptocurrency holdings.

Stablecoins and Yield Farming: Creating Incentives

Stablecoins, cryptocurrencies pegged to traditional assets like the US Dollar, became a cornerstone of the DeFi ecosystem. They provided stability in a highly volatile environment, enabling users to navigate the DeFi landscape without being exposed to the price fluctuations of other cryptocurrencies. Yield farming, a practice where users "farm" yield by providing liquidity to DeFi protocols, became an innovative way to earn returns on cryptocurrency holdings.

Challenges and Vulnerabilities: Navigating Complexity

While DeFi presented an exciting opportunity for disruption, it was not without its challenges. The complexity of smart contracts and the need for secure coding practices introduced vulnerabilities that bad actors were quick to exploit. Auditing, a critical practice for ensuring the security of DeFi protocols, sometimes fell short, leading to rugpulls and loss of funds.

Mainstream Recognition and Adoption

As DeFi platforms gained traction, they attracted the attention of both individual investors and institutional players. The promise of decentralized and permissionless finance resonated with those looking to diversify their portfolios and explore new investment opportunities. The DeFi movement began to bridge the gap between the crypto community and the broader financial industry.

Conclusion: A Glimpse of the Future

The birth of DeFi marked a pivotal moment in the evolution of blockchain technology. It showed that decentralized principles could extend beyond simple transactions and challenge the very foundations of traditional finance. As we proceed through this chapter, exploring the vulnerabilities and rugpull incidents within the

DeFi landscape, it's essential to remember the transformative potential that inspired its creation. The promise of a more inclusive, transparent, and accessible financial system provided the backdrop against which the complexities of the DeFi world unfolded.

Smart Contract Vulnerabilities: Explore the technical vulnerabilities within DeFi smart contracts that led to rugpulls.

The decentralized finance (DeFi) movement revolutionized the financial landscape by introducing a new paradigm of permissionless and automated financial services. At the heart of this innovation were smart contracts – self-executing code that enabled the creation of sophisticated financial instruments. However, the intricate nature of smart contracts also introduced vulnerabilities that malicious actors exploited, resulting in rugpull incidents. This chapter delves into the technical flaws within DeFi smart contracts that led to these rugpulls, examining the root causes, the impact on the ecosystem, and the lessons they conveyed.

The Smart Contract Revolution: Pioneering Automated Agreements

Smart contracts held the promise of automating agreements and transactions in a trustless and transparent manner. Ethereum's introduction of smart contracts in 2015 unleashed a wave of creativity, spawning DeFi platforms that offered lending, borrowing, trading, and yield farming. However, the complexity of coding these contracts meant that vulnerabilities could emerge, sometimes leading to unintended and harmful consequences.

The Code is Law: Immutable Yet Fragile

One of the core principles of smart contracts is immutability – once deployed, the code cannot be altered. While this ensured transparency and predictability, it also meant that any vulnerabilities or errors present in the code remained unchangeable. This dichotomy of immutability and vulnerability created a precarious situation where a single coding mistake could have devastating consequences.

The DAO Hack: A Watershed Moment

The Decentralized Autonomous Organization (DAO) hack of 2016 served as a stark reminder of the vulnerabilities in smart contracts. A flaw in the DAO's code allowed an attacker to drain a substantial portion of the organization's funds. While the hack led to a contentious hard fork to reverse the damage, it highlighted the need for rigorous code auditing and the potential for financial havoc in DeFi platforms.

Reentrancy Attacks: Draining Vulnerabilities

Reentrancy attacks emerged as a common vulnerability within DeFi smart contracts. These attacks exploit a contract's vulnerability to recursive calls, allowing attackers to drain funds repeatedly before the contract can update its state. The notorious reentrancy attack on the Ethereum-based lending platform "bZx" in 2020 showcased how a single vulnerability could be exploited to manipulate markets and cause significant financial losses.

Unchecked User Inputs: The Vulnerability of Trust

Smart contracts often rely on data provided by external sources, known as oracles, to make decisions. If these inputs are not properly validated, malicious actors can manipulate them to trigger unintended outcomes. The "flash loan" attack on the lending protocol "dForce" demonstrated how manipulated user inputs could be exploited to drain a platform's funds.

Complexity Breeds Vulnerability: Over-Engineering and Bugs

The complexity of DeFi smart contracts often led to over-engineering, where layers of complexity masked underlying vulnerabilities. Bugs in these intricate contracts could go unnoticed until they were exploited. A bug in the "YAM" protocol's rebase mechanism illustrated how a single coding mistake could render a project's token worthless.

Copy-Paste Code: A Recipe for Disaster

The open-source nature of blockchain projects encouraged collaboration and innovation. However, it also led to a practice of copy-pasting code from other projects without proper understanding or customization. This approach introduced vulnerabilities that were present in the original codebase, propagating weaknesses across multiple projects.

The Domino Effect: Cascading Vulnerabilities

The interconnected nature of DeFi protocols meant that vulnerabilities in one contract could propagate through the ecosystem, leading to a cascade of failures. Flash loan attacks and other vulnerabilities exposed how a single exploit could trigger a series of events that affected multiple platforms.

Lessons in Security and Preparedness

The rugpull incidents stemming from smart contract vulnerabilities served as wake-up calls for the DeFi ecosystem. Projects began to recognize the necessity of thorough code audits, rigorous testing, and constant monitoring. Bug bounty programs and community-driven audits became essential tools in preventing vulnerabilities.

Conclusion: Navigating the Technical Terrain

The exploration of smart contract vulnerabilities highlights the paradox of innovation and risk within the DeFi landscape. As DeFi platforms continue to advance and introduce novel features, they must grapple with the challenge of maintaining robust security practices. As we continue our journey through this chapter, exploring the impact of rugpull incidents and their aftermath, the vulnerabilities within smart contracts will remain a critical backdrop for understanding the complexities of maintaining trust and security in the DeFi realm.

Lessons in Code and Trust: Understand the importance of robust coding and trustless systems in DeFi projects.

The decentralized finance (DeFi) movement brought forth a vision of reshaping the financial landscape through innovative applications built on blockchain technology. At the heart of these applications were smart contracts, self-executing pieces of code that automated financial interactions. However, the rugpull incidents that emerged within the DeFi ecosystem underscored the critical importance of robust coding practices and the concept of trustlessness. This chapter delves into the lessons learned about the significance of robust coding and trustless systems in DeFi projects, shedding light on the intricate interplay between technology, security, and user confidence.

The Allure of Smart Contracts: From Vision to Reality

Smart contracts promised to revolutionize the way financial transactions and agreements were executed. By removing intermediaries and enabling automation, they opened up a world of possibilities for DeFi applications. However, the successful implementation of these contracts hinged on the integrity of the code and the trust placed in the underlying system.

Robust Coding: The Foundation of Trust

The development of DeFi smart contracts requires meticulous attention to coding practices. Rigorous code reviews, audits, and testing are essential to identify and rectify vulnerabilities before they can be exploited. The vulnerabilities revealed by rugpull incidents underscored that even a seemingly small oversight in code could lead to catastrophic consequences.

Code Audits and Security Checks: A Necessity, Not a Luxury

The rugpull incidents served as a wakeup call for the DeFi ecosystem, highlighting the need for comprehensive code audits. Independent audits by expert firms became standard practice, providing a second pair of eyes to identify potential vulnerabilities. This external scrutiny aimed to instill confidence in users, investors, and the wider community.

Smart Contract Complexity: A Double-Edged Sword

The complexity of DeFi smart contracts is both a testament to innovation and a potential source of vulnerabilities. While these contracts can automate intricate financial agreements, the complexity also means that potential vulnerabilities may remain hidden. Balancing complexity with simplicity in coding became a crucial consideration for DeFi developers.

The Importance of Open Source and Transparency

The open-source nature of blockchain projects encourages collaboration and transparency. However, it also requires vigilance in ensuring that the shared codebase is secure. Transparency in development and decision-making processes fosters trust among users, enabling the community to actively contribute to identifying and mitigating vulnerabilities.

Decentralization and the Trustless Paradigm

The concept of "trustlessness" is at the core of blockchain technology. DeFi projects aimed to create systems where users could engage in transactions and agreements without having to trust intermediaries. However, the rugpull incidents raised questions about whether these systems truly achieved the desired level of trustlessness.

Oracles and External Data Sources: A Weak Link

Decentralized applications often rely on oracles to provide external data necessary for smart contracts to execute. However, the integrity of these data sources became a potential weak link, as inaccuracies or manipulation could lead to unintended outcomes. Addressing this challenge required careful design and validation.

The Role of Governance and Upgrades

DeFi projects often include governance mechanisms that allow token holders to participate in decision-making processes and upgrades. While this decentralization of governance can enhance user engagement, it also demands careful consideration of security measures to prevent malicious manipulation of voting and upgrade processes.

Community Vigilance and Shared Responsibility

The rugpull incidents reinforced the notion that security is a collective responsibility. The DeFi community began to collaborate on identifying vulnerabilities, sharing insights, and raising awareness about potential risks. This community-driven vigilance aimed to prevent future rugpull incidents and strengthen the overall security of the ecosystem.

Conclusion: A Call to Balance

The DeFi ecosystem learned valuable lessons from the rugpull incidents, reiterating that innovation and security must go hand in hand. The significance of robust coding, diligent auditing, and fostering trustless systems became clear as the DeFi landscape evolved. As we proceed through this chapter, exploring the impact of rugpull incidents and their aftermath, the lessons learned about code and trust will remain a foundational backdrop for understanding the complexities of maintaining security and user confidence within the DeFi realm.

Chapter 3: The Great ICO Gold Rush
ICO Frenzy: Dive into the Initial Coin Offering (ICO) mania and the promise of easy fundraising for crypto projects.

The evolution of cryptocurrencies introduced not only new ways of transacting value but also novel methods of raising capital for innovative projects. The Initial Coin Offering (ICO) emerged as a groundbreaking fundraising mechanism that promised to democratize investment opportunities and provide a pathway for projects to realize their visions. This chapter delves into the ICO frenzy, examining its origins, the mechanics behind it, the allure it held for both investors and entrepreneurs, and the eventual challenges and vulnerabilities that emerged.

The Birth of the ICO: A Disruptive Fundraising Paradigm

As cryptocurrencies gained traction, visionary entrepreneurs saw an opportunity to revolutionize traditional funding models. The ICO was born as a means of raising funds by issuing tokens on a blockchain, granting investors ownership in the project or access to its services. This concept departed from traditional venture capital or initial public offerings (IPOs), allowing projects to raise capital directly from a global pool of investors.

ICO Mechanics: Tokenization and Distribution

The ICO process typically involved the creation of tokens representing a stake in the project or utility within its ecosystem. These tokens were then distributed to investors who participated in the ICO by contributing cryptocurrencies like Bitcoin or Ethereum. The tokens were often issued as a form of a smart contract on a blockchain, enabling automated distribution and ownership verification.

The Allure of ICOs: Democratization of Investment

The ICO frenzy promised a democratization of investment opportunities that was previously unavailable through traditional fundraising methods. Investors from around the world, regardless of their geographic location or financial status, could participate in funding early-stage projects. This opened doors for retail investors and enthusiasts who wanted to support projects aligned with their interests.

A New Era of Innovation: Diverse Project Verticals

The ICO boom saw projects spanning a wide spectrum of industries – from blockchain infrastructure and financial services to gaming, healthcare, and more. This diverse range of projects showcased the versatility of the ICO model and its potential to disrupt traditional sectors.

ICO Investment Mechanics: Speculation and Hype

While some investors believed in the long-term potential of ICO projects, others saw them as opportunities for short-term gains. The speculative nature of ICO investing led to a sense of urgency and a "Fear Of Missing Out" (FOMO) mentality, which sometimes fueled inflated valuations and an emphasis on token price appreciation.

The Promise of Liquidity: Secondary Markets and Token Exchanges

Investors were drawn to the liquidity promise associated with ICO tokens. Unlike traditional startup investments, ICO tokens could be traded on secondary markets and token exchanges shortly after the completion of the ICO. This liquidity option added an additional layer of attraction for investors looking to capitalize on short-term price movements.

The Unregulated Landscape: Lack of Investor Protections

The ICO frenzy was characterized by a lack of regulatory oversight and investor protections. While this allowed for innovation and rapid fundraising, it also exposed investors to risks. Fraudulent projects, misleading whitepapers, and even well-intentioned projects with inadequate execution plans contributed to a market rife with uncertainty.

Challenges and Vulnerabilities: The Dark Side of ICOs

As the ICO market grew, challenges and vulnerabilities emerged. Investors faced the risk of investing in projects that lacked proper due diligence, transparent roadmaps, or viable use cases. The influx of capital into ICO projects also attracted malicious actors who saw opportunities to exploit investor enthusiasm and trust.

ICO Mania Peaks and Subsides: Lessons Learned

The ICO frenzy reached its zenith in 2017 and early 2018, with billions of dollars raised for projects globally. However, as the landscape matured, issues like regulatory scrutiny, a lack of accountability, and numerous scams came to light. The market eventually corrected, leading to a recalibration of expectations and a shift toward more sustainable fundraising models.

Conclusion: The ICO Legacy

The ICO frenzy reshaped the landscape of fundraising and investment. It introduced new avenues for innovation, enabling projects to secure capital directly from their communities. However, it also exposed the vulnerabilities and challenges inherent in an unregulated and speculative environment. As we navigate through the rest of this chapter, examining the darker aspects of the ICO era, it's essential to remember the optimism and potential that fueled this groundbreaking fundraising mechanism and its enduring impact on the broader cryptocurrency ecosystem.

The Rise of Scams: Expose the deceptive ICO projects that exploited investors' excitement and trust.

The Initial Coin Offering (ICO) craze brought with it a surge of innovative projects and investment opportunities. However, the promise of easy fundraising also attracted malicious actors who sought to exploit the excitement and trust of eager investors. This chapter delves into the darker side of the ICO era, unveiling the deceptive ICO projects that surfaced, their tactics, the impact they had on the ecosystem, and the lessons they left in their wake.

The Proliferation of Deceptive Projects: A Dark Underbelly

As ICOs gained popularity, a wave of fraudulent projects emerged, capitalizing on the exuberance and lack of regulatory oversight. These deceptive projects aimed to deceive investors through false promises, misleading information, and fabricated narratives. The exponential growth of the ICO market created fertile ground for these scams to thrive.

Misleading Whitepapers: Crafting Illusions of Success

Deceptive ICO projects often produced whitepapers that painted an enticing picture of innovation and potential returns. These whitepapers, while sophisticated in appearance, often lacked substance or technical depth. Malicious actors exploited investors' lack of technical expertise, using complex jargon to create an illusion of legitimacy.

Fictitious Teams and Stolen Identities

Fraudulent ICOs frequently presented fictional or exaggerated team members, complete with fake profiles and photos. In some cases, they even stole identities of legitimate individuals to establish credibility. Investors were lured by charismatic team descriptions and fabricated backgrounds, further blurring the lines between reality and deception.

Unrealistic Roadmaps and Overambitious Goals

Deceptive projects often set unrealistic goals and timelines, promising rapid development and adoption. These overambitious roadmaps were designed to captivate investors with the promise of massive returns, leading them to disregard the practical challenges of executing complex projects within the proposed timeframes.

Faux Partnerships and Nonexistent Alliances

To bolster their credibility, some fraudulent ICOs claimed partnerships with established companies or associations. These partnerships were often invented or exaggerated, creating a facade of legitimacy. Investors who trusted these claims were left disillusioned when these partnerships failed to materialize.

Phantom Advisors and Influencers

Deceptive ICOs employed tactics to associate themselves with well-known industry figures, advisors, or influencers. These individuals, often unaware of their false endorsements, inadvertently lent credibility to scams. This manipulation exploited the trust investors placed in respected voices within the cryptocurrency space.

Pump and Dump Schemes: Orchestrating Price Manipulation

A subset of deceptive ICOs engaged in "pump and dump" schemes, artificially inflating the value of their tokens through coordinated marketing efforts. Once the price reached a certain level, the malicious actors behind the scheme would sell their holdings, causing the token's value to plummet and leaving genuine investors with significant losses.

Exit Scams: Vanishing Act of Deceptive Projects

Perhaps the most devastating form of ICO deception was the exit scam, where projects that had successfully raised funds disappeared entirely after the ICO. These malicious actors absconded with investors' contributions, leaving behind only empty promises and shattered dreams.

Investor Fallout: Erosion of Trust and Confidence

The prevalence of deceptive ICO projects eroded investors' trust and confidence in the broader cryptocurrency ecosystem. As victims shared their stories and experiences, the community became more cautious, questioning the legitimacy of even well-intentioned projects. The fallout from these scams cast a shadow over the entire ICO landscape.

The Regulatory Response: Navigating the Wild West

As the deception within the ICO market became more apparent, regulators started taking notice. Governments and agencies worldwide began to issue warnings and guidelines, aiming to protect investors from fraudulent schemes. The regulatory response marked a shift toward a more accountable and regulated fundraising landscape.

Lessons Learned: Vigilance and Due Diligence

The deceptive ICO projects left a lasting legacy of caution and vigilance within the cryptocurrency community. Investors learned the importance of conducting thorough due diligence, scrutinizing whitepapers, verifying team identities, and seeking third-party audits. The scams became a stark reminder that, while the promise of innovation was real, it was essential to navigate the space with a critical eye.

Conclusion: A Bittersweet Era

The rise of scams within the ICO frenzy was a bittersweet chapter in the cryptocurrency saga. While the ICO era ushered in innovation and democratized fundraising, it also exposed investors to manipulation and deception. As we delve deeper into this chapter, exploring the vulnerabilities and repercussions of deceptive ICO projects, it's crucial to remember the lessons learned and the efforts made to ensure a more transparent and secure investment landscape in the future.

Regulatory Vacuum: Discuss the lack of regulatory guidance and how it contributed to the proliferation of scams.

The Initial Coin Offering (ICO) frenzy brought with it an era of innovation and promise, but it also exposed a vulnerability that would shape the landscape for years to come – the lack of regulatory guidance. As the ICO market soared, a regulatory vacuum allowed scams and fraudulent projects to flourish. This chapter delves into the absence of effective regulatory oversight during the ICO era, discussing its origins, the challenges it posed, the vulnerabilities it exposed, and the eventual regulatory response.

The Wild West of Finance: A Lack of Clear Guidelines

The early days of the ICO market were characterized by a lack of comprehensive regulatory guidance. Cryptocurrencies and blockchain technology were relatively new concepts, and regulators struggled to keep pace with the rapid evolution of the industry. This lack of clear guidelines created an environment where projects could operate without substantial oversight, opening the door to both innovation and abuse.

Innovators vs. Bad Actors: Navigating Gray Areas

The absence of regulatory clarity led to a blurred line between legitimate innovators and malicious actors. While some projects were genuinely striving to bring new ideas to fruition, others exploited the regulatory vacuum to launch scams, exploiting investors' enthusiasm and trust. The lack of a standardized framework made it challenging for investors to distinguish between the two.

Token Classification Dilemma: Security or Utility?

One of the most significant regulatory challenges during the ICO era was determining whether tokens should be classified as securities or utility tokens. The classification held significant legal and regulatory implications. Projects sought to position their tokens as utilities to avoid the stringent requirements associated with securities, leading to regulatory uncertainty.

The Scam Proliferation: A Breeding Ground for Deception

The lack of regulatory guidance provided fertile ground for deceptive ICO projects to proliferate. Malicious actors exploited the absence of standards and accountability, preying on investors' excitement and trust. Fraudulent projects saw an opportunity to raise funds without adhering to the rigorous standards of traditional fundraising methods.

An Avalanche of Whitepapers: Innovation or Manipulation?

With minimal regulatory oversight, the ICO market saw an influx of whitepapers promising revolutionary ideas and technologies. However, the absence of standardized disclosure requirements allowed deceptive projects to publish whitepapers filled with inflated claims and misleading information. This further muddied the waters for investors seeking credible projects.

Investor Vulnerability: Navigating an Uncharted Landscape

The regulatory vacuum left investors in an unfamiliar and potentially treacherous environment. Investors lacked the protections and safeguards that traditional financial systems provided. Scammers leveraged this vulnerability, orchestrating elaborate schemes to exploit the lack of oversight and accountability.

Erosion of Trust and Reputation: Fallout from Deception

As fraudulent ICO projects proliferated, investor trust in the broader cryptocurrency ecosystem eroded. The lack of regulatory guidance contributed to the perception that the market was rife with scams and unreliable projects. This erosion of trust had far-reaching implications for both the ICO market and the broader adoption of blockchain technology.

The Need for Regulation: A Call for Clarity

The rise of scams and fraudulent projects within the ICO market prompted a growing demand for regulatory intervention. Investors, industry participants, and even some projects recognized the need for clear guidelines to differentiate between legitimate projects and scams. The absence of regulation hindered the maturation of the industry and stifled its potential.

Regulatory Responses: A Shift Towards Accountability

As the negative consequences of the regulatory vacuum became more evident, governments and regulatory bodies began to take action. Some countries introduced measures to curb the proliferation of scams, while others sought to provide clarity on the legal status of tokens. These efforts marked a turning point toward a more regulated and accountable ICO landscape.

Lessons Learned: Balancing Innovation and Oversight

The lack of regulatory guidance during the ICO era served as a cautionary tale about the balance between innovation and regulatory oversight. The proliferation of scams underscored the importance of maintaining investor protection, ensuring transparency, and fostering an environment where legitimate projects could thrive.

Conclusion: A Regulatory Awakening

The regulatory vacuum that defined the ICO era had profound implications for the cryptocurrency industry. As we navigate through the remainder of this chapter, exploring the impact of scams and the regulatory response, it's crucial to remember that the lessons learned from this period continue to shape the regulatory landscape for cryptocurrencies and blockchain technology. The challenges faced during the ICO gold rush underscored the need for clear guidelines and responsible oversight to foster a more secure and trustworthy ecosystem.

Chapter 4: Hacking and Exploits

The Dark Side of Crypto: Investigate high-profile hacks and exploits that targeted early crypto exchanges and projects

The emergence of cryptocurrencies promised a new era of financial empowerment and security. However, alongside the potential benefits, the digital nature of cryptocurrencies also attracted malicious actors seeking to exploit vulnerabilities for personal gain. This chapter delves into the darker aspects of the crypto space, exploring high-profile hacking incidents and exploits that targeted early crypto exchanges and projects. By examining the methods employed by hackers, the impact on the ecosystem, and the lessons learned, we uncover the challenges of securing digital assets in a borderless and decentralized environment.

The Crypto Attraction: A Hacking Playground

The decentralized and pseudonymous nature of cryptocurrencies initially attracted hackers seeking opportunities to exploit technical vulnerabilities and weak security measures. The allure of potentially large payouts, coupled with the anonymity afforded by cryptocurrencies, prompted hackers to develop sophisticated techniques to breach the security of crypto exchanges and projects.

Early Crypto Exchanges: A Lucrative Target

In the early days of cryptocurrencies, exchanges served as the primary entry points for users to convert fiat currency into digital assets. Their centrality to the ecosystem made them prime targets for hackers. By infiltrating exchanges, hackers could gain access to vast amounts of users' digital assets, wreaking havoc on both individuals and the overall market.

The Mt. Gox Saga: A Watershed Moment

The notorious hacking incident involving Mt. Gox in 2014 was a defining moment for the crypto community. The Tokyo-based exchange, once the largest in the world, suffered a catastrophic breach resulting in the loss of approximately 850,000 bitcoins. This incident not only highlighted the vulnerabilities of early exchanges but also underscored the need for improved security practices and regulatory oversight.

Exchange Vulnerabilities: Techniques Exploited

Hackers employed various techniques to compromise the security of exchanges. These included exploiting coding vulnerabilities, conducting Distributed Denial of Service (DDoS) attacks to overwhelm servers, and utilizing social engineering tactics to trick employees into revealing sensitive information.

Smart Contract Exploits: Vulnerabilities in Code

The rise of blockchain platforms with programmable smart contracts introduced a new vector for exploitation. Smart contracts, while powerful, were prone to coding errors that could be manipulated by malicious actors. The DAO hack, which exploited a vulnerability in a smart contract, demonstrated the potential for devastating consequences.

Ripple Effects: The Impact on Trust and Confidence

High-profile hacking incidents had far-reaching effects on investor trust and market sentiment. The loss of user funds eroded confidence in both the affected exchanges and the broader cryptocurrency ecosystem. These incidents exposed the challenges of maintaining security in an industry built on decentralization and privacy.

Regaining Trust: Crisis Management and Recovery

In the aftermath of hacking incidents, affected exchanges faced the daunting task of regaining user trust and compensating for losses. Some exchanges chose to reimburse affected users, while others implemented security upgrades and more rigorous auditing processes to prevent future breaches.

The Evolution of Hacks: From Heists to Ransomware

As the cryptocurrency landscape evolved, hacking techniques also advanced. The emergence of ransomware attacks, where hackers encrypt user data and demand cryptocurrency payments in exchange for decryption, added a new layer of complexity to the threat landscape.

A Shared Responsibility: User Education and Security Measures

The wave of hacking incidents underscored the importance of user education and personal security measures. Crypto users needed to understand the risks of storing assets on exchanges and adopt practices such as cold storage and two-factor authentication to mitigate potential threats.

Lessons Learned: A Call for Vigilance

The high-profile hacking incidents targeting early crypto exchanges and projects taught the industry valuable lessons about the importance of security, transparency, and collaboration. These incidents highlighted the need for continuous security audits, penetration testing, and proactive risk mitigation measures.

Conclusion: A Quest for Cyber Resilience

The exploration of high-profile hacks and exploits within the crypto space reveals the harsh reality of digital asset security in a borderless and decentralized environment. As we journey through the remainder of this chapter, examining the vulnerabilities and aftermath of hacking incidents, it's essential to recognize the collective efforts made to enhance cybersecurity and fortify the industry against future attacks. The pursuit of cyber resilience remains an ongoing endeavor as the crypto ecosystem matures and adapts to an ever-evolving threat landscape.

Security Breaches: Analyze the weak points in exchange platforms and project infrastructures that were exploited.

The rise of cryptocurrencies brought with it a wave of innovation and potential, but it also exposed vulnerabilities that hackers eagerly exploited. This chapter delves into the heart of cyber insecurity, examining the security breaches that targeted exchange platforms and project infrastructures within the early cryptocurrency ecosystem. By dissecting the weak points that hackers targeted, the tactics they employed, and the consequences of their actions, we gain insight into the ongoing challenges of safeguarding digital assets and maintaining trust within a decentralized environment.

Exchange Platforms: The Center of Attention

Cryptocurrency exchanges stood at the forefront of the digital asset landscape, serving as hubs for trading, investment, and conversion between traditional and digital currencies. The pivotal role they played made them prime targets for hackers seeking to compromise security systems, access user funds, and disrupt market stability.

Centralization vs. Decentralization: A Double-Edged Sword

The centralization inherent to many exchange platforms offered convenience and accessibility for users but also concentrated the potential impact of security breaches. In contrast, decentralized exchanges aimed to mitigate these risks by allowing users to retain control of their private keys and trade directly from their wallets.

The Anatomy of Hacks: Weak Points Exploited

Hacking incidents against exchange platforms often exploited a combination of technical, operational, and human vulnerabilities. These weak points included inadequate security measures, poor risk management, lack of transparency, and unsuspecting staff members who fell prey to social engineering tactics.

Technical Vulnerabilities: Coding Errors and Exploitable Flaws

Hackers frequently exploited coding errors and software vulnerabilities within exchange platforms. These ranged from insecure APIs (Application Programming Interfaces) to faulty implementation of security protocols. By exploiting these technical weaknesses, hackers could gain unauthorized access to sensitive systems and user data.

Operational Lapses: Neglecting Best Practices

Inadequate operational practices, such as poor patch management, weak encryption, and insufficient network monitoring, opened the door for hackers to infiltrate exchange platforms. In some cases, exchanges neglected to implement basic security measures, leaving them susceptible to a wide range of attacks.

Social Engineering: The Human Element

Hackers recognized the power of exploiting human vulnerabilities through social engineering tactics. Phishing attacks, where hackers impersonated legitimate entities to steal sensitive information, played a significant role in compromising exchange security. Unsuspecting staff members could inadvertently provide access to sensitive systems or data.

Compromised Hot Wallets: The Perfect Heist

Hot wallets, used by exchanges to facilitate rapid withdrawals, became attractive targets for hackers due to their accessibility. Breaching an exchange's hot wallet meant gaining access to a significant amount of digital assets, which could then be laundered or moved to external accounts.

The Ripple Effect: Impact on Users and Market Sentiment

Hacking incidents against exchange platforms had profound consequences for users and the broader market. Users faced the loss of their digital assets, and the resulting loss of trust undermined investor confidence in the entire ecosystem. Market sentiment often suffered, leading to fluctuations in cryptocurrency prices.

A Continuous Battle: Staying Ahead of Hackers

The evolving tactics of hackers kept exchange platforms and project teams in a constant state of vigilance. As security measures improved, hackers adapted and developed new methods to compromise systems. This ongoing battle highlighted the need for continuous security assessments and rapid response protocols.

Lessons Learned: Security as a Priority

The security breaches that plagued exchange platforms and project infrastructures emphasized the critical importance of cybersecurity within the cryptocurrency ecosystem. The lessons learned included the necessity of robust encryption, multi-factor authentication, regular security audits, and a proactive approach to risk management.

Conclusion: Striving for Cyber Resilience

The exploration of security breaches within the cryptocurrency landscape underscores the inherent challenges of safeguarding digital assets in an environment where innovation and vulnerability coexist. As we proceed through this chapter, dissecting the implications and aftermath of these breaches, it's essential to recognize the industry's collective efforts to bolster security measures and build a more resilient ecosystem. The quest for cyber resilience remains an ongoing journey as the cryptocurrency space evolves and adapts to an ever-changing threat landscape.

Repercussions on Trust: Examine how hacking incidents affected investor trust in the safety of the crypto space.

The early cryptocurrency ecosystem promised a revolution in financial freedom and security. However, the frequent occurrence of hacking incidents targeting exchange platforms and projects undermined this promise, shaking the foundations of trust that the industry was built upon. This chapter delves into the aftermath of high-profile hacking incidents, exploring the profound impact these breaches had on investor trust in the safety of the crypto space. By analyzing the psychological and market effects, as well as the industry's response, we gain insight into the challenges of rebuilding confidence in a decentralized and rapidly evolving landscape.

The Trust Paradigm: A Cornerstone of Adoption

Trust is the bedrock on which any financial system is built. In the cryptocurrency world, where transactions occur across digital channels and personal interaction is limited, trust takes on heightened importance. Investors rely on the security of exchange platforms and projects to protect their assets and provide a sense of stability.

Shattered Illusions: The Fallout of Hacking Incidents

The occurrence of high-profile hacking incidents shattered the illusions of security and invulnerability that initially characterized the crypto space. When exchanges and projects suffered breaches, investors faced the harsh reality that their digital assets were not as secure as they believed. The impact of this revelation rippled through the market, leading to a crisis of confidence.

Market Volatility and Investor Panic

Hacking incidents often triggered immediate market volatility as news of breaches spread. The sudden dumping of compromised assets by hackers, combined with panic selling by worried investors, led to rapid price drops. These price fluctuations further eroded investor trust and created an atmosphere of uncertainty.

Reputation Damage: Exchange Platforms and Beyond

Hacking incidents not only damaged the reputation of the targeted exchanges but also cast a shadow over the entire industry. Negative headlines, stories of financial loss, and images of frustrated investors resonated with the broader public, associating cryptocurrencies with insecurity and scams.

Trust as a Scarce Resource: The Psychological Impact

Investor psychology played a significant role in the aftermath of hacking incidents. Many investors experienced a loss of trust not only in the specific exchanges or projects that were breached but also in the broader cryptocurrency ecosystem. The fear of future breaches and potential losses impacted investment decisions and attitudes toward digital assets.

The Industry's Response: Rebuilding Trust

As the implications of hacking incidents became apparent, the industry recognized the need to address the crisis of confidence. Exchange platforms and projects began implementing enhanced security measures, conducting audits, and communicating openly with users to regain trust. The collective efforts aimed to demonstrate a commitment to safeguarding assets and improving transparency.

Security Audits and Transparency: A New Norm

The increase in security audits and transparent communication became central to restoring trust. Exchange platforms and projects started sharing information about their security practices, measures taken to prevent future breaches, and steps they were undertaking to compensate affected users.

Lessons from Hacks: Strengthening the Ecosystem

Despite the damage wrought by hacking incidents, the lessons learned prompted positive change within the crypto ecosystem. The emphasis on security led to the development of new technologies, protocols, and practices designed to fortify the industry against future breaches.

Building Trust Through Regulation and Accountability

The regulatory response to hacking incidents played a crucial role in rebuilding trust. As governments introduced measures to regulate exchanges and provide user protections, investors gained a sense of security knowing that the industry was being held accountable.

Conclusion: The Struggle for Trust in a Digital Age

The exploration of the repercussions of hacking incidents on investor trust highlights the fragility of trust in a digital age. As we delve deeper into the complexities of post-breach dynamics, it's essential to recognize the steps taken by the industry to address the crisis and restore confidence. The journey toward rebuilding trust is ongoing, reflecting the resilience of the crypto community as it navigates the challenges of security, transparency, and trust in an evolving landscape.

Chapter 5: Social Engineering and Manipulation Psychological Tactics: Uncover the methods used by scammers to manipulate public perception and promote fraudulent projects.

In the intricate world of cryptocurrencies, where digital assets and decentralized networks intersect with human psychology, scammers have capitalized on the vulnerabilities of human behavior to advance their deceitful agendas. This chapter delves into the realm of psychological manipulation, exploring the methods employed by scammers to manipulate public perception and promote fraudulent projects. By dissecting the intricate web of tactics used, the impact on individuals and the broader crypto community, we gain insight into the complexity of social engineering within the crypto space.

The Power of Perception: Leveraging Psychological Vulnerabilities

Scammers recognize that human psychology is a powerful tool to exploit. They exploit cognitive biases, emotions, and decision-making processes to create a perception of legitimacy and opportunity where none exists. By understanding these psychological vulnerabilities, scammers can influence investors' behaviors and decisions.

Creating Illusion: The Trustworthy Persona

Scammers often craft a façade of trustworthiness by creating fake personas, including team members and advisors. These personas are designed to evoke feelings of familiarity, credibility, and reliability, all of which play on individuals' innate need to trust and connect with others.

FOMO and the Fear of Missing Out

The Fear Of Missing Out (FOMO) is a psychological phenomenon where individuals fear losing out on potential opportunities and experiences. Scammers exploit FOMO by creating a sense of urgency and scarcity, suggesting that immediate action is necessary to seize an incredible opportunity.

Building Emotional Connections: The Halo Effect

Scammers aim to build emotional connections with potential victims by appealing to their emotions and aspirations. The Halo Effect, a cognitive bias where positive traits in one area influence perceptions of an individual's overall character, is exploited to portray scammers as altruistic, innovative, or revolutionary.

Psychological Anchoring: Influencing Perceived Value

Anchoring is a cognitive bias where people rely heavily on the first piece of information they receive when making decisions. Scammers use this bias to manipulate the perceived value of their projects by anchoring them to an inflated valuation, leading investors to believe they are getting a bargain.

Leveraging Social Proof: The Bandwagon Effect

The Bandwagon Effect is the tendency for people to do something primarily because others are doing it. Scammers create a sense of social proof by showcasing fictitious testimonials, endorsements from influential figures, and manipulated metrics to give the illusion of widespread adoption and success.

Eliciting Trust Through Authority: Authority Bias

Authority bias is the tendency to attribute greater accuracy to the opinion of an authority figure. Scammers manipulate this bias by falsely claiming endorsements from industry experts, advisors, and well-known figures to gain trust and credibility.

Exploiting Cognitive Biases: Confirmation Bias and Selective Perception

Confirmation bias is the tendency to interpret information in a way that confirms one's preexisting beliefs. Scammers take advantage of this bias by selectively presenting information that supports their narrative and avoiding facts that might raise doubts.

Implications for the Crypto Community: Skepticism and Vigilance

Scammers' psychological tactics have far-reaching implications for the crypto community. Individuals must remain vigilant and critically evaluate information, even when it aligns with their beliefs. Building a culture of skepticism and due diligence becomes essential to counteract the influence of manipulative tactics.

Countering Manipulation: Educating the Community

Education becomes a powerful weapon against manipulation. By equipping the crypto community with knowledge about psychological tactics and providing tools to critically assess projects and claims, individuals can make informed decisions and resist manipulation.

Conclusion: Navigating the Psychological Minefield

As we unravel the intricate web of psychological tactics employed by scammers within the crypto space, it's imperative to recognize the complexity of the challenge at hand. The exploration of these methods shines a light on the vulnerabilities that exist at the intersection of human psychology and digital assets. Moving forward, the crypto community's ability to counter manipulation rests on the foundation of education, skepticism, and vigilance, ensuring that individuals can navigate this psychological minefield with awareness and resilience.

FOMO and FUD: Explore how Fear Of Missing Out (FOMO) and Fear, Uncertainty, and Doubt (FUD) were leveraged to influence the market.

In the dynamic world of cryptocurrencies, emotions often play a pivotal role in shaping market behavior. Scammers and manipulators leverage these emotions to create artificial narratives that influence investor decisions and market trends. This chapter delves into the concepts of Fear Of Missing Out (FOMO) and Fear, Uncertainty, and Doubt (FUD), uncovering how these psychological tactics were harnessed to manipulate perceptions, drive actions, and influence the trajectory of the crypto market. By examining the mechanics of FOMO and FUD, their effects on investor behavior, and the ways the crypto community can guard against their influence, we gain insight into the power of emotions within the digital asset landscape.

Emotion as a Market Catalyst: FOMO and FUD Unveiled

Emotions are intrinsically tied to investment decisions. FOMO and FUD represent two distinct but equally potent emotions that scammers and manipulators have capitalized on to sway market sentiments and outcomes.

Fear Of Missing Out (FOMO): The Urgency to Participate

FOMO is a psychological phenomenon where individuals fear missing out on potentially rewarding experiences or opportunities. Scammers exploit FOMO by creating a sense of urgency, implying that immediate action is required to secure incredible gains or be part of a groundbreaking venture.

Creating Urgency: Orchestrating FOMO

Scammers orchestrate FOMO by fabricating scenarios where time is of the essence. They might announce limited-time investment opportunities, introduce countdowns, or suggest that a project is on the verge of a massive breakthrough. These tactics manipulate investors into making hasty decisions driven by a fear of missing out on lucrative prospects.

The Ripple Effect: FOMO's Impact on Prices

FOMO-driven actions can have a cascading effect on cryptocurrency prices. As investors scramble to buy into a perceived hot investment, demand surges, often leading to price spikes. However, these spikes can be short-lived, and when reality sets in, prices may experience dramatic reversals.

Fear, Uncertainty, and Doubt (FUD): Planting Seeds of Doubt

FUD is a tactic that aims to spread doubt and uncertainty to undermine confidence in a project or the market as a whole. Scammers employ FUD to create panic, sow seeds of doubt about a project's credibility, or even insinuate a looming crisis to drive prices down.

Manufacturing Uncertainty: Crafting FUD Campaigns

Scammers craft FUD campaigns by disseminating negative information, unfounded rumors, or half-truths. These campaigns can include spreading news of regulatory crackdowns, alleged vulnerabilities in projects, or exaggerated risks associated with specific investments.

Exploiting Cognitive Biases: Anchoring and Negativity Bias

Anchoring bias, where people rely heavily on initial information, and negativity bias, where negative information holds more weight than positive, both play into FUD campaigns. Scammers anchor investors' perceptions with negative information, making it harder for them to disregard negative claims.

Market Impact: FUD's Effect on Prices and Sentiments

FUD campaigns can cause short-term panic, leading to rapid price drops. These campaigns exploit investors' fears, prompting them to sell assets in anticipation of losses.

Additionally, FUD can create a climate of uncertainty, resulting in decreased market participation and stunted growth.

Guarding Against Manipulation: Education and Critical Thinking

Recognizing the power of FOMO and FUD is crucial for individual investors and the broader crypto community. Education and critical thinking play pivotal roles in countering these tactics. By understanding the psychological mechanisms at play and remaining informed, investors can make more rational and well-informed decisions.

Industry Responsibility: Transparency and Communication

Exchange platforms, project teams, and influential figures bear a responsibility to communicate transparently and responsibly. Transparent disclosures, timely updates, and proactive debunking of false information can help counteract FUD campaigns and maintain market stability.

Conclusion: Emotions in the Crypto Arena

As we navigate the intricate web of emotions within the crypto landscape, it's essential to recognize the impact of FOMO and FUD on investor behavior and market trends. By unraveling these psychological tactics, we gain insight into the power of emotions and the challenges they present.

Moving forward, the ability of individuals and the community to guard against manipulation rests on fostering a culture of informed decision-making, skepticism, and emotional resilience within a rapidly evolving and emotionally charged market.

The Human Factor: Discuss the role of social engineering and human vulnerabilities in facilitating rugpulls.

In the ever-evolving landscape of cryptocurrencies, scams and rugpulls have become unfortunate realities. One of the most potent tools in the scammers' arsenal is social engineering—a practice that exploits human psychology and vulnerabilities to manipulate individuals into making decisions that benefit the manipulator. This chapter delves into the complex realm of social engineering, examining how it facilitates rugpulls and undermines trust within the crypto community. By dissecting the tactics used, the psychological mechanisms at play, and the ways individuals and the community can guard against these techniques, we gain insight into the intricate interplay between human nature and digital assets.

The Anatomy of Social Engineering: Exploiting Human Psychology

Social engineering leverages human psychology to deceive and manipulate. By exploiting cognitive biases, emotions, and the innate desire for trust and connection, scammers engineer scenarios that compel victims to take actions against their best interests.

The Power of Trust: The Foundation of Social Engineering

Trust is central to human interactions. Scammers exploit this inherent need by creating scenarios that evoke feelings of trust and credibility. They impersonate trusted figures, fabricate endorsements, and concoct narratives that resonate with victims' aspirations and values.

Creating a False Sense of Urgency: Urgency Bias

Urgency bias is a psychological phenomenon where people prioritize immediate actions over more considered decisions. Scammers exploit this bias to induce individuals to act hastily without fully evaluating the situation. Rugpulls often capitalize on urgency by convincing victims that they must act immediately to avoid missing out.

Appealing to Emotions: Emotional Manipulation

Emotional manipulation is a core component of social engineering. Scammers use emotions such as fear, greed, and excitement to cloud rational judgment. Rugpulls exploit this by generating emotional responses that prompt victims to disregard warning signs and make impulsive decisions.

Leveraging Social Proof: The Bandwagon Effect

The Bandwagon Effect, where people conform to the actions of others, plays a crucial role in social engineering. Scammers create a sense of social proof by presenting fake testimonials, exaggerated success stories, and manipulated metrics, pushing victims to join the perceived trend.

Baiting the Hook: The Psychology of Phishing

Phishing is a form of social engineering that targets victims through digital communication. Scammers create authentic-looking messages that evoke trust and prompt recipients to reveal sensitive information or transfer funds. Rugpulls often involve phishing tactics to compromise victims' wallets.

The Psychology of Influence: The Role of Authority

Scammers manipulate the principle of authority to establish credibility. By claiming endorsements from experts, advisors, or influencers, they trigger the Authority Bias, causing victims to trust their claims without thorough verification.

Victim Blaming and Shame: Exploiting Cognitive Dissonance

Cognitive dissonance occurs when individuals hold contradictory beliefs or behaviors. Scammers exploit this by convincing victims that their losses are a result of their own mistakes, inducing feelings of shame and discouraging them from seeking help.

Preying on Hope: Optimism Bias

Optimism bias is the tendency for people to believe that positive events are more likely to happen to them than negative events. Scammers use this bias to foster a sense of hope, even when faced with obvious red flags, and to manipulate victims into overlooking potential risks.

Guarding Against Manipulation: Awareness and Education

Recognizing the tactics of social engineering is paramount for individuals and the crypto community. Education and awareness serve as the first line of defense against rugpulls. By understanding these techniques and regularly practicing skepticism, individuals can better protect themselves from falling victim.

Collective Defense: Community Vigilance

The crypto community plays a vital role in guarding against social engineering. By sharing information about potential scams, reporting suspicious activities, and fostering a culture of collaboration, the community can collectively thwart the efforts of scammers.

Conclusion: Navigating the Complexities of Trust and Deception

As we navigate the intricate interplay between human vulnerabilities and rugpulls within the crypto landscape, it's essential to recognize the power of social engineering in manipulating individuals' decisions and actions. The exploration of these tactics underscores the importance of skepticism, critical thinking, and education. Moving forward, the crypto community's ability to protect itself against manipulation lies in fostering a culture of awareness, empowerment, and resilience in the face of evolving deceptive practices.

Chapter 6: Learning from Mistakes

Community Responses: Witness how the crypto community rallied to expose and learn from rugpull incidents.

The cryptocurrency community is a dynamic and resilient network of individuals who share a common passion for innovation and financial sovereignty. When rugpull incidents—the deceptive schemes that prey on investors' trust—threaten the integrity of the ecosystem, the crypto community often responds with determination and unity. This chapter dives into the heart of the community's responses, exploring how it rallies to expose rugpull incidents, confront scammers, and learn from its mistakes. By delving into the mechanisms of collaboration, vigilance, and knowledge-sharing, we gain insight into how a community driven by decentralized ideals works collectively to safeguard the integrity of the crypto space.

The Crypto Community: A Network of Vigilance

The decentralized nature of cryptocurrencies extends to the community itself. It's not just individuals, but a network of vigilant participants who understand the importance of safeguarding the ecosystem against malicious actors.

Empowerment Through Transparency: Whistleblowers and Watchdogs

Whistleblowers play a critical role in exposing rugpull incidents. These brave individuals come forward with evidence, revealing the inner workings of scams and fraudulent projects. Online forums, social media groups, and dedicated watchdog organizations offer platforms for whistleblowers to share their findings.

Unveiling the Web of Deceit: Collaborative Investigations

Community members often collaborate to investigate suspicious projects and individuals. They pool resources, share insights, and work collectively to uncover fraudulent activities. By leveraging a variety of skills and perspectives, they expose scams that might otherwise go unnoticed.

The Power of Data: Analyzing Suspicious Activity

Data analysis plays a vital role in exposing rugpulls. Community members scrutinize transaction histories, blockchain data, and project documentation to identify irregularities and inconsistencies. By analyzing patterns, they uncover the true nature of fraudulent schemes.

The Watchful Eye: Community-Driven Due Diligence

Due diligence extends beyond individual investors. Community members research and analyze projects before investing time, money, or trust. They examine whitepapers, team backgrounds, and project goals, sharing insights and cautionary advice with fellow enthusiasts.

Raising Alarms: Public Awareness Campaigns

When evidence of rugpulls surfaces, the community launches public awareness campaigns to inform others. Social media, online forums, and cryptocurrency news outlets become platforms for disseminating information, urging caution, and encouraging thorough research.

The Call to Action: Reporting and Vigilance

Reporting suspicious activities to relevant authorities is a vital step in tackling rugpulls. Community members collaborate with regulatory agencies and law enforcement to ensure scammers are held accountable for their actions.

Turning the Tide: Knowledge-Sharing and Education

As rugpull incidents are exposed and dissected, the crypto community learns valuable lessons. These lessons are shared through articles, tutorials, and webinars, empowering others to recognize and avoid similar scams in the future.

Creating a Resilient Ecosystem: Building Together

The collective responses of the crypto community underscore its commitment to creating a resilient and secure ecosystem. By actively engaging in discussions, sharing insights, and remaining vigilant, community members contribute to building an environment where scams are less likely to thrive.

Rising Stronger: The Evolution of Community Responses

Over time, the crypto community's responses to rugpull incidents have evolved. It has become more organized, strategic, and proactive in identifying and combating scams. As the community learns from its mistakes, its collective knowledge grows, making it increasingly difficult for scammers to exploit vulnerabilities.

Conclusion: Unity in the Face of Adversity

The exploration of how the crypto community rallies to expose and learn from rugpull incidents highlights the unity and resilience inherent in this ecosystem. The community's responses not only safeguard individual investors but also contribute to the larger goal of a trustworthy and secure crypto landscape. As we move forward, the collective vigilance and collaboration within the community will remain critical components in preventing and addressing future rugpull incidents, reinforcing the decentralized ideals that underpin the world of cryptocurrencies.

Improved Due Diligence: Understand how investors and projects began adopting better due diligence practices.

As the cryptocurrency landscape continues to evolve, the scars left by rugpull incidents have not gone unnoticed. These incidents, fueled by deception and manipulation, have prompted introspection within the crypto community. Both investors and project teams have recognized the need for heightened vigilance and thorough research before engaging with any project. This chapter delves into the realm of improved due diligence, exploring how the lessons learned from rugpulls have led to the adoption of more stringent evaluation practices. By dissecting the mechanisms of due diligence, its impact on decision-making, and the ways it has transformed the crypto ecosystem, we gain insight into the evolution of a more cautious and informed approach to engagement.

Redefining Due Diligence: A Response to Deception

The fallout from rugpull incidents revealed significant gaps in the due diligence practices of both investors and project teams. Improved due diligence emerged as a natural response to mitigate risks and build a more secure foundation for the crypto space.

From Blind Trust to Critical Examination: The Shift in Mindset

Rugpulls shattered the notion that projects should be taken at face value. Investors began to realize that a more skeptical approach was necessary. Rather than blindly trusting promises, they started demanding transparency, accountability, and verifiable information.

Thoroughly Scrutinizing Projects: A Comprehensive Approach

Investors became more proactive in researching projects before committing their funds. Whitepapers, project goals, team backgrounds, and technical roadmaps are now subjected to intense scrutiny. The availability of online resources, forums, and dedicated websites further empowers investors to gather information.

Learning from Red Flags: Identifying Warning Signs

The patterns and warning signs of rugpulls have become lessons for the community. Investors now look for inconsistencies, vague promises, lack of transparency, and overly ambitious claims as red flags. By identifying these signs early on, they can steer clear of potential scams.

Engaging the Community: Collective Wisdom

The crypto community has evolved into a valuable resource for investors seeking information about projects.

Online forums, social media groups, and community-driven due diligence efforts provide a platform for sharing insights, discussing red flags, and conducting preliminary investigations.

Transparency as a Pillar: Project Teams Respond

The onus of transparency lies with project teams as well. Those who recognized the importance of trust began to provide clearer and more comprehensive information about their projects. Transparent documentation, open communication, and regular updates became standard practices.

Learning from Mistakes: Honesty About Past Failures

Project teams that have learned from mistakes embraced transparency by sharing their experiences, even when things did not go as planned. This honesty demonstrated growth and commitment, fostering trust within the community.

Education and Awareness: Fostering Informed Investors

Improved due diligence extends beyond individual projects. The crypto community has taken on the responsibility of educating newcomers about the importance of due diligence. Through articles, guides, and workshops, newcomers are equipped with the tools to make informed decisions.

Regulatory Influence: Compliance and Investor Protection

Regulatory developments have also contributed to improved due diligence. Regulations that hold projects accountable for the accuracy of their claims and the protection of investors have incentivized transparency and due diligence as a means of compliance.

Conclusion: A More Informed Crypto Ecosystem

The journey from rugpull incidents to improved due diligence signifies a maturing crypto ecosystem. The lessons learned have transformed how investors engage with projects, emphasizing skepticism, transparency, and collective vigilance. The shift toward more stringent due diligence practices reflects the resilience of the community and its commitment to building a secure and trustworthy crypto landscape. As the crypto ecosystem continues to evolve, the lessons from rugpull incidents will serve as a lasting reminder of the importance of informed decision-making and critical examination.

Building Resilience: Explore the steps taken to fortify the crypto ecosystem against future rugpulls.

Rugpull incidents have left an indelible mark on the cryptocurrency ecosystem, igniting a collective drive to strengthen its foundations against deceptive practices. The crypto community, project teams, and even regulators have taken proactive steps to build resilience, enhance transparency, and safeguard investors. This chapter delves into the realm of building resilience, examining the strategies employed to fortify the crypto ecosystem against future rugpulls. By dissecting regulatory measures, technological innovations, community-driven initiatives, and industry collaborations, we gain insight into how the crypto world is forging a path toward a more secure and resilient future.

Regulatory Evolution: Crafting a Framework for Transparency

Regulatory bodies worldwide have recognized the need to protect investors from rugpulls and scams. They are crafting frameworks that require projects to adhere to disclosure standards, ensure transparency, and provide accurate information about their operations.

Licensing and Compliance: Setting Standards

Regulators are introducing licensing and compliance requirements for cryptocurrency projects. These measures compel projects to meet certain criteria, undergo audits, and adhere to transparency standards, reducing the potential for fraudulent activities.

Investor Protection: Ensuring Accountability

Regulations are increasingly emphasizing investor protection. Projects must provide clear documentation, risk disclosures, and disclaimers, ensuring that investors are well-informed about potential risks before committing their funds.

Technological Safeguards: Innovations to Counter Deception

Technological innovations are playing a pivotal role in fortifying the crypto ecosystem against rugpulls. From advanced blockchain analytics to identity verification solutions, these tools are creating new layers of security.

Blockchain Analytics: Tracing Suspicious Activities

Blockchain analytics platforms are becoming more sophisticated in identifying suspicious transactions and patterns. These tools help uncover hidden connections, track fund flows, and identify potential scams.

Smart Contract Audits: Preventing Vulnerabilities

Smart contract vulnerabilities are often exploited in rugpull incidents. To counter this, specialized audit firms review and verify smart contracts, identifying potential flaws and vulnerabilities before they can be exploited.

Decentralized Identity Solutions: KYC and AML Measures

Decentralized identity solutions are enhancing Know Your Customer (KYC) and Anti-Money Laundering (AML) measures. These tools allow projects to verify the identities of participants and ensure compliance with regulatory requirements.

Community-Led Vigilance: Crowdsourced Security

The crypto community has embraced a proactive role in safeguarding the ecosystem. Platforms that allow users to collectively report and analyze projects have emerged, creating a shared knowledge base to help identify potential scams.

Early Detection and Reporting: Real-Time Monitoring

Real-time monitoring of projects and transactions helps detect suspicious activities early. Community members, investors, and platforms collaborate to report and investigate anomalies promptly.

Collaborative Initiatives: Industry Alliances

Industry alliances, collaborations, and partnerships are forming to tackle rugpull incidents collectively. These alliances pool resources, share information, and work toward common goals of transparency and investor protection.

Education as Armor: Empowering the Masses

Education remains one of the most potent weapons against rugpulls. The crypto community is actively engaging in education initiatives to empower investors with knowledge, enabling them to make informed decisions.

Conclusion: Forging a Resilient Future

The steps taken to fortify the crypto ecosystem against future rugpulls reflect a dynamic and multifaceted approach. Regulatory measures, technological innovations, community-driven initiatives, and industry collaborations together create a robust defense against deceptive practices. The journey from rugpull incidents to a more resilient future underscores the resilience of the crypto community and its commitment to learning from mistakes. As the crypto ecosystem continues to evolve, the efforts to build resilience will remain at the forefront, ensuring a safer and more secure environment for investors and participants alike.

Chapter 7: Regulation on the Horizon

The Call for Regulation: Delve into the debates surrounding the need for regulatory oversight in the crypto world.

The rapid rise of cryptocurrencies and decentralized technologies has ushered in a transformative era in finance and technology. Alongside the innovation, however, has come an increasing recognition of the need for regulatory oversight within the crypto space. This chapter delves into the complex debates surrounding the call for regulation, examining the arguments for and against regulatory intervention in the crypto world. By dissecting the concerns, potential benefits, and challenges associated with regulatory oversight, we gain insight into the intricate interplay between innovation, security, and the need for a balanced regulatory framework.

The Crypto Landscape: A Double-Edged Sword of Innovation

Cryptocurrencies and blockchain technology have introduced unprecedented levels of innovation and potential for financial democratization. However, the very qualities that make these technologies revolutionary—decentralization, anonymity, and lack of intermediaries—

have also raised concerns about security, legality, and potential abuse.

The Argument for Regulation: Mitigating Risks and Ensuring Compliance

Protecting Investors: Advocates for regulation assert that clear rules and guidelines can safeguard investors from scams, fraudulent projects, and rugpulls. By providing transparency and enforcing accountability, regulation can help establish trust and credibility within the crypto ecosystem.

Consumer Protection: The absence of regulations can expose consumers to risks, as they lack legal recourse in case of disputes. Regulatory oversight can ensure that products and services adhere to certain standards, promoting consumer confidence.

Anti-Money Laundering (AML) and Counter-Terrorism Financing (CTF): Regulatory measures can help prevent the misuse of cryptocurrencies for illegal activities, such as money laundering and funding terrorism. AML and CTF regulations require entities to identify their customers and report suspicious transactions.

Market Integrity and Stability: Without regulation, the crypto market can be susceptible to manipulation and extreme volatility. Regulatory measures can promote market stability by curbing fraudulent practices and ensuring fair trading practices.

The Argument Against Regulation: Preserving Decentralization and Innovation

Innovation at Risk: Some argue that excessive regulation could stifle innovation by imposing bureaucratic hurdles on startups and developers. The flexible and open nature of the crypto space allows for experimentation and rapid development.

Decentralization and Freedom: The very essence of cryptocurrencies lies in their decentralized nature, allowing individuals to transact and participate without intermediaries. Advocates for minimal regulation fear that overreach could compromise this fundamental aspect.

Regulatory Lag and Adaptability: The pace of technological innovation often outstrips the ability of traditional regulatory frameworks to adapt. Critics worry that rigid regulations might become outdated or fail to address emerging challenges effectively.

Privacy and Autonomy: Striking a balance between regulatory oversight and individuals' privacy rights is challenging. Some fear that stringent regulations could infringe on individuals' financial autonomy and privacy.

The Path Forward: Striking a Balance

Balancing Security and Innovation: Finding the right balance between fostering innovation and ensuring security is a complex task. Regulation must aim to protect investors and participants without stifling technological progress.

Global Coordination: The borderless nature of cryptocurrencies requires global coordination in regulatory efforts. Collaborative approaches can prevent regulatory arbitrage and create consistent standards across jurisdictions.

Gradual and Informed Regulation: Advocates suggest that regulation should evolve gradually, informed by a deep understanding of the crypto ecosystem. Regulatory bodies must actively engage with industry stakeholders to develop effective measures.

Educating Regulators: Effective regulation requires regulators to comprehend the nuances of the crypto world. Education initiatives can bridge the gap between regulators' understanding and the complexities of decentralized technologies.

Conclusion: Navigating the Regulatory Landscape

The call for regulation within the crypto world sparks complex debates that cut to the core of innovation, security, and individual autonomy. Striking the right balance between fostering innovation and ensuring investor protection remains a challenge. As the crypto space continues to evolve, the discussions surrounding regulatory oversight will play a pivotal role in shaping the future of cryptocurrencies, blockchain technologies, and the broader financial landscape.

Early Efforts: Examine the first attempts at implementing regulatory measures to curb rugpulls.

As the cryptocurrency landscape matures, the need for regulatory oversight becomes increasingly evident. The rising tide of rugpull incidents and fraudulent activities has prompted regulatory bodies around the world to take action. This chapter delves into the early efforts to implement regulatory measures to curb rugpulls, exploring the challenges, successes, and lessons learned from the initial stages of regulatory intervention. By dissecting the strategies, motivations, and impacts of these early regulatory initiatives, we gain insight into the evolution of the crypto regulatory landscape and its ongoing mission to foster security and trust within the ecosystem.

The Regulatory Landscape: Navigating New Territory

The unique characteristics of cryptocurrencies and the decentralized nature of blockchain technology pose novel challenges for regulators. Crafting effective regulatory measures requires an understanding of the nuances of the crypto world while balancing innovation with investor protection.

The Drive for Clarity: The Motivation Behind Early Regulatory Efforts

Investor Protection: The primary motivation for early regulatory efforts was to protect investors from fraudulent activities, scams, and rugpull incidents. Regulators recognized the need to establish guidelines that promote transparency, accountability, and trust within the crypto ecosystem.

Preventing Financial Crimes: Early regulatory measures aimed to curb money laundering, terrorist financing, and other illegal activities facilitated by cryptocurrencies. Regulators sought to implement Anti-Money Laundering (AML) and Know Your Customer (KYC) procedures to bring the crypto world in line with established financial norms.

Curbing Market Manipulation: Market manipulation and insider trading posed significant threats to the integrity of the crypto market. Regulators aimed to develop measures that prevent price manipulation and ensure fair trading practices.

Challenges of Jurisdiction: The Global Nature of Cryptocurrencies

The borderless nature of cryptocurrencies complicates the implementation of regulatory measures. Early regulatory efforts faced challenges in defining jurisdiction, harmonizing regulations across jurisdictions, and coordinating cross-border enforcement.

Diverse Approaches: A Glimpse into Early Regulatory Measures

Licensing and Registration: Some regulatory bodies introduced licensing and registration requirements for crypto businesses and projects. These measures aimed to ensure that only legitimate and transparent projects could operate within their jurisdiction.

Disclosure and Transparency: Regulators emphasized the need for clear disclosure of project information, financial statements, and potential risks. Transparent documentation allowed investors to make informed decisions.

AML and KYC Compliance: To prevent money laundering and other illicit activities, regulators required crypto exchanges and service providers to implement AML and KYC procedures. This approach aimed to create a paper trail that could be traced back to participants.

Market Surveillance: Regulators began monitoring cryptocurrency markets for suspicious activities and price manipulation. This surveillance helped identify irregularities and protect investors from fraudulent trading practices.

Lessons Learned: The Evolution of Regulation

Adaptation and Flexibility: Early regulatory efforts taught regulators the importance of remaining adaptable and open to feedback. The dynamic nature of the crypto world required regulators to evolve their approaches in response to emerging challenges.

Global Collaboration: As early regulatory measures were implemented, the need for global collaboration became evident. Collaborative efforts between regulatory bodies and international organizations are essential to creating consistent and effective regulatory standards.

Balancing Innovation and Protection: The delicate balance between fostering innovation and protecting investors remains a key consideration. Regulators must strike a balance that supports technological progress while ensuring security and transparency.

Conclusion: Pioneering Steps Toward Regulation

The examination of the first attempts at implementing regulatory measures to curb rugpulls highlights the evolving nature of the crypto regulatory landscape. While early efforts faced challenges, they laid the foundation for a more secure and accountable crypto ecosystem. The lessons learned from these early regulatory initiatives will continue to guide the development of effective regulatory frameworks that foster trust, transparency, and innovation within the crypto world.

Striking the Balance: Discuss the challenges of regulating a decentralized and global industry.

The call for regulatory oversight in the cryptocurrency ecosystem has gained momentum, driven by the need to protect investors, ensure market integrity, and foster innovation. However, the path to effective regulation is rife with challenges, especially in a landscape characterized by decentralization and global reach. This chapter delves into the intricacies of striking the balance between regulation and innovation, exploring the complex challenges that regulators face when attempting to govern a decentralized and borderless industry. By dissecting the hurdles, potential solutions, and the ongoing efforts to harmonize regulatory approaches, we gain insight into the multifaceted nature of crypto regulation and its role in shaping the future of finance and technology.

Decentralization's Dilemma: Regulation and Autonomy

The Essence of Decentralization: Cryptocurrencies and blockchain technology are built on the principles of decentralization, which prioritizes autonomy, transparency, and the absence of intermediaries. This ethos clashes with traditional regulatory models that rely on central authority.

Preserving Innovation: Striking the right balance between regulation and innovation is crucial. Overregulation could stifle creativity and experimentation, limiting the potential for groundbreaking technological advancements.

Security vs. Privacy: Regulating decentralized technologies requires navigating the delicate balance between ensuring security and safeguarding individuals' privacy and autonomy.

Global Reach, Local Jurisdictions: Regulatory Complexity

Jurisdictional Challenges: The borderless nature of cryptocurrencies makes jurisdictional boundaries blurred. Cryptocurrency transactions can occur across multiple jurisdictions simultaneously, complicating efforts to enforce regulations.

Diverse Legal Frameworks: Different countries have varying legal frameworks for cryptocurrencies, from outright bans to embrace and integration. Regulators must navigate this diverse landscape to create effective regulations.

Regulatory Arbitrage: Projects and participants might relocate to jurisdictions with more lenient regulations, undermining the effectiveness of stricter regulatory approaches.

Adapting to Technological Pace: Regulation and Innovation

Technological Lag: Traditional regulatory frameworks often lag behind the pace of technological innovation, leading to regulatory uncertainty and gaps in oversight.

Innovative Complexity: Regulators must understand complex technologies like smart contracts, decentralized applications, and privacy-enhancing tools to effectively regulate them.

Balancing Transparency and Anonymity:

Transparency and Accountability: Effective regulation requires transparency and accountability. Regulators need to balance these requirements with the privacy and pseudonymity that cryptocurrencies offer.

User-Centric Approaches: Striking the right balance involves understanding that user needs and preferences are diverse. Some users value privacy and pseudonymity, while others seek security and accountability.

Education and Collaboration: Bridging the Gap

Regulator Education: Educating regulators about the intricacies of decentralized technologies is vital to crafting effective and fair regulations. Industry engagement and knowledge-sharing can bridge this education gap.

Collaboration with Industry: Regulators and industry stakeholders need to collaborate to develop regulations that strike the right balance. Industry expertise can inform effective regulatory approaches.

International Coordination: Given the global nature of the cryptocurrency ecosystem, international collaboration is key. Standardized regulations and shared best practices can minimize regulatory arbitrage.

Conclusion: A Balanced Future

Navigating the challenges of regulating a decentralized and global industry requires careful consideration, collaboration, and an understanding of both technological nuances and regulatory complexities. The path to striking the right balance is a complex journey, as regulators aim to harness the potential of cryptocurrencies and blockchain technology while safeguarding investors and maintaining market integrity. The ongoing efforts to harmonize regulatory approaches, educate stakeholders, and promote international cooperation pave the way for a balanced future where innovation thrives within a secure and accountable crypto ecosystem.

Conclusion

The Evolution of Crypto: Reflect on how the early years shaped the trajectory of the crypto space.

The journey through the intricacies of rugpull incidents, regulatory developments, and the evolution of the cryptocurrency ecosystem has provided a comprehensive understanding of the challenges and triumphs that have shaped the trajectory of this revolutionary space. As we conclude this exploration, it is imperative to reflect on the transformative power of the early years and the lasting impact they have had on the world of finance, technology, and beyond. This concluding chapter delves into the evolution of crypto, analyzing the pivotal role played by rugpull incidents in shaping the industry's growth, resilience, and maturity. By dissecting the lessons learned, the advances made, and the challenges that remain, we gain insight into the lasting legacy of the early years and the path forward for cryptocurrencies and decentralized technologies.

From Naiveté to Awareness: Rugpull Incidents as Catalysts

The rugpull incidents that punctuated the early years of the crypto world served as wake-up calls for participants, highlighting the importance of due diligence, transparency, and vigilance. These incidents demonstrated that while cryptocurrencies offered unprecedented opportunities, they also required responsible engagement.

Cultivating Resilience and Trust

The rugpull incidents forced the crypto community to evolve and adapt. From demanding transparency and accountability to developing improved due diligence practices, the community transformed its approach to project evaluation. This shift towards resilience and vigilance has laid the foundation for a more secure and trustworthy crypto ecosystem.

Regulation as a Response to Vulnerability

The rise of rugpull incidents accelerated the call for regulatory oversight. Governments and regulatory bodies recognized the need to protect investors, curtail fraudulent activities, and establish a framework that fosters trust and stability. Early regulatory efforts have set the stage for ongoing discussions about how to regulate a decentralized and innovative industry.

Technology's Triumph: Innovations Born from Challenges

The rugpull incidents also spurred technological advancements aimed at enhancing security and accountability within the crypto space. Blockchain analytics, smart contract audits, and decentralized identity solutions are among the tools that emerged in response to the vulnerabilities exposed by rugpulls.

The Crypto Community's Metamorphosis: Learning and Collaboration

Rugpull incidents prompted the crypto community to become more educated, informed, and collaborative. Online forums, social media groups, and community-driven due diligence efforts created a support network for investors and a platform for sharing insights. The collective response to rugpull incidents highlighted the community's resilience and determination to learn from its mistakes.

A Global Endeavor: Regulation and International Cooperation

The global nature of the cryptocurrency ecosystem has made regulation a complex and multifaceted endeavor. The debates surrounding regulation reflect the challenge of balancing innovation and investor protection across diverse legal frameworks and jurisdictions. International cooperation has become crucial in ensuring consistent regulatory standards.

The Unfinished Tapestry: Challenges and Aspirations

While the crypto ecosystem has made significant strides since the early years, challenges persist. Regulatory frameworks continue to evolve, seeking to strike the delicate balance between fostering innovation and ensuring investor protection. Technological advancements continue to drive the industry forward, but with them come new vulnerabilities and risks.

Looking Forward: A Secure and Inclusive Future

The journey through the rugpull incidents, regulatory developments, and technological innovations ultimately points toward a future where cryptocurrencies and decentralized technologies play an integral role in global finance and technology. The lessons learned from the early years serve as a guide for building a more secure, transparent, and inclusive crypto ecosystem.

Embracing the Lessons: Moving Forward with Caution and Confidence

As we close the chapter on rugpull incidents and their impact, it is clear that the crypto community has learned from its past and is actively working towards a better future. The trajectory of the crypto space, shaped by the experiences of the early years, is one of growth, maturity, and adaptability. While challenges remain, the path forward is defined by the resilience, innovation, and determination that have become hallmarks of the cryptocurrency ecosystem. As cryptocurrencies continue to redefine the boundaries of finance and technology, the lessons from rugpull incidents will remain embedded in the foundation of a secure and prosperous crypto future.

Lessons for the Future: Summarize the key takeaways and cautionary lessons from the era of rugpulls.

The era of rugpulls within the cryptocurrency landscape has been a crucible of challenges, revelations, and transformation. As we bring our journey to a close, it is essential to distill the essence of the lessons learned and the cautionary tales that will guide the path forward. This concluding chapter encapsulates the key takeaways from the rugpull incidents, offering a comprehensive overview of the insights gained, the vulnerabilities exposed, and the wisdom acquired during this pivotal period. By dissecting these lessons for the future, we illuminate the road ahead for cryptocurrencies, decentralized technologies, and the global community that embraces their potential.

Lesson 1: Vigilance and Due Diligence

Rugpull incidents underscore the importance of thorough due diligence before investing in or participating in any crypto project. This lesson emphasizes that a healthy skepticism and a commitment to research are critical for identifying red flags, fraudulent activities, and unreliable projects.

Lesson 2: Transparency and Accountability

Transparency and accountability lie at the heart of a resilient crypto ecosystem. Projects that prioritize open communication, clear documentation, and regular updates build trust with their communities. Investors, in turn, should demand transparency and hold projects accountable for their promises.

Lesson 3: Regulatory Evolution

The regulatory landscape is evolving, and compliance with regulatory measures is becoming paramount for legitimacy and sustainability. The lesson here is that a healthy collaboration between projects, regulators, and the crypto community is essential for creating effective regulatory frameworks that balance innovation and investor protection.

Lesson 4: Technological Maturity

Technological innovation is a double-edged sword. While it brings immense possibilities, it also exposes vulnerabilities. The lesson here is that robust coding practices, continuous security audits, and proactive efforts to fix vulnerabilities are vital for the health of smart contracts, decentralized applications, and the overall crypto infrastructure.

Lesson 5: Empowerment through Education

Knowledge is power in the crypto space. Educated participants are better equipped to identify scams, assess risks, and make informed decisions. The lesson here is that fostering a culture of education, learning, and information sharing within the crypto community is crucial for long-term success.

Lesson 6: Community Resilience and Collaboration

The crypto community's resilience in the face of rugpull incidents is commendable. A united front against scams, fraud, and deception enhances collective security. The lesson here is that fostering collaboration, supporting community-driven initiatives, and sharing insights can mitigate risks and promote a more transparent ecosystem.

Lesson 7: Balancing Innovation and Security

Innovation and security must coexist. Striking the right balance ensures that progress isn't hindered by excessive regulations, while also safeguarding participants from undue risks. The lesson here is that maintaining a delicate equilibrium between pushing boundaries and ensuring safety is crucial for the long-term viability of the crypto space.

Lesson 8: A Global Perspective

Cryptocurrencies transcend geographical boundaries, necessitating a global perspective. International collaboration, harmonized regulatory standards, and cross-border partnerships are essential for creating a cohesive and secure crypto ecosystem. The lesson here is that the crypto community's global nature demands a united effort to address challenges and shape the future.

Lesson 9: Constant Adaptation

The crypto landscape is dynamic, with new challenges emerging regularly. Lessons learned from rugpull incidents should serve as a foundation for continuous adaptation, learning, and growth. The lesson here is that a commitment to ongoing improvement and the willingness to adapt to changing circumstances are essential traits for success.

Lesson 10: The Essence of Resilience

Rugpull incidents, while painful, have acted as crucibles of resilience. They have revealed the determination of the crypto community to learn from mistakes, collaborate, and progress. The lesson here is that resilience is a cornerstone of the crypto space, enabling participants to weather challenges and emerge stronger.

Conclusion: Navigating the Future with Wisdom

As we draw the curtain on the era of rugpulls, the lessons learned will continue to guide the trajectory of cryptocurrencies, blockchain technology, and the wider decentralized ecosystem. The crypto community's ability to learn from its past mistakes, adapt to new challenges, and collaborate to build a more secure and transparent environment is a testament to its resilience. Armed with the insights gained from rugpull incidents, participants in the crypto space are poised to shape a future that is characterized by responsible innovation, heightened security, and the collective pursuit of a more inclusive and trustworthy global financial landscape.

The Road Ahead: Look forward to a more resilient and secure future for cryptocurrencies and decentralized finance.

The Road Ahead: Looking Forward to a More Resilient and Secure Future for Cryptocurrencies and Decentralized Finance

As we conclude this journey through rugpull incidents, regulatory developments, and the evolution of the cryptocurrency ecosystem, the path forward beckons with promise and potential. The lessons learned, challenges confronted, and triumphs celebrated have laid the groundwork for a future that embraces the ideals of security, innovation, and responsible engagement. This concluding chapter delves into the road ahead for cryptocurrencies and decentralized finance, offering a forward-looking perspective on how the crypto community, regulators, and innovators can collaborate to shape a landscape that is not only resilient but also built on a foundation of trust, transparency, and empowerment.

A Blueprint for Resilience: Lessons Translated into Action

The lessons extracted from rugpull incidents serve as a blueprint for fostering resilience within the crypto ecosystem. By applying the principles of due diligence, transparency, and accountability, projects and participants can create an environment that resists fraudulent activities and safeguards investor interests.

Technological Evolution: Enhancing Security and Efficiency

Technological advancements continue to propel the crypto space forward. Innovations such as multi-signature wallets, decentralized identity solutions, and improved smart contract auditing tools are reshaping the landscape by enhancing security, user experience, and project reliability.

Decentralized Finance's Ascension: Unlocking Financial Inclusion

Decentralized finance (DeFi) has emerged as a transformative force, offering a decentralized alternative to traditional financial services. As DeFi projects continue to evolve, the focus on security, user education, and transparent governance will be crucial for achieving broader financial inclusion and resilience.

Collaboration as a Catalyst: Industry and Regulatory Partnership

The crypto industry's collaboration with regulatory bodies is pivotal for achieving a harmonious balance between innovation and investor protection. Regulatory frameworks that acknowledge the unique features of cryptocurrencies and blockchain technology will create an environment where both security and progress flourish.

Global Cooperation: Harmonizing Regulatory Approaches

The global nature of the crypto ecosystem requires international cooperation to harmonize regulatory approaches. Through shared best practices, regulatory standards, and cross-border collaborations, the crypto world can build a framework that ensures consistency and minimizes regulatory arbitrage.

Empowering Users: Financial Education and Literacy

Empowering users with financial education and literacy is a cornerstone of a secure crypto ecosystem. By understanding risks, opportunities, and best practices, participants can make informed decisions that safeguard their investments and contribute to a healthier crypto environment.

Innovation with Responsibility: Navigating Emerging Technologies

As emerging technologies like decentralized autonomous organizations (DAOs), non-fungible tokens (NFTs), and cross-chain interoperability gain traction, responsible innovation becomes paramount. Projects must prioritize security audits, transparency, and clear governance mechanisms to ensure their viability.

Sustainability and Longevity: Shaping the Crypto Legacy

The crypto community's legacy will be defined by its commitment to sustainability and longevity. Sustainability in terms of technological progress, investor protection, and ethical practices will contribute to a resilient ecosystem that endures beyond short-term trends.

Championing Trust: Every Participant's Responsibility

Building trust within the crypto space is a collective endeavor. It requires every participant, from developers to investors, to prioritize ethical conduct, transparency, and accountability. Trust is the bedrock upon which a resilient crypto ecosystem can thrive.

Conclusion: A Resilient Future Built Together

The journey through rugpull incidents, regulatory milestones, and technological advancements offers a glimpse into the transformative power of the cryptocurrency landscape. As we venture into the road ahead, the crypto community stands at a crossroads—a juncture where lessons learned can be transformed into action, where innovation can be coupled with responsibility, and where security can coexist with progress.

The future of cryptocurrencies and decentralized finance is not without challenges, but it is one defined by the resilience, adaptability, and determination that the community has consistently demonstrated. By learning from the past and embracing the opportunities of tomorrow, the crypto ecosystem can foster a future that embodies the values of trust, security, and empowerment. As we collectively contribute to the evolution of this revolutionary landscape, we pave the way for a world where financial inclusivity, innovation, and responsible engagement define a legacy that transcends time and transcends borders.

THE END

Wordbook

Welcome to the glossary section of this book. Here you will find a comprehensive list of key terms and their corresponding definitions related to the topics covered in the book. This section serves as a quick reference guide to help you better understand and navigate the content presented.

1. Rugpulls: A rugpull refers to a fraudulent act where the creators of a cryptocurrency project or token suddenly abandon the project, often after accumulating a significant amount of funds from investors, leaving the investors with worthless or significantly devalued assets.

2. Cryptocurrency: A digital or virtual form of currency that uses cryptography for secure transactions, control of new units, and verification of asset transfers on a decentralized network, typically based on blockchain technology.

3. Decentralization: The distribution of control and decision-making authority across a network or system, where no single entity has absolute power. In the context of cryptocurrencies, decentralization refers to the absence of a central authority governing transactions and data.

4. Crypto Community: The collective network of individuals, developers, investors, and enthusiasts who

participate in the cryptocurrency ecosystem, including discussions, collaborations, and investment activities.

5. Altcoins: Alternative cryptocurrencies to Bitcoin. Altcoins encompass a wide range of digital currencies other than Bitcoin, each with its own features, use cases, and underlying technologies.

6. Decentralized Finance (DeFi): A category of financial services and applications built on blockchain technology that aims to provide traditional financial services, such as lending, borrowing, trading, and asset management, in a decentralized and permissionless manner.

7. Initial Coin Offering (ICO): An early-stage fundraising method in which a new cryptocurrency project offers tokens or coins to investors in exchange for funding. ICOs were popular during the early years of the crypto industry.

8. Regulation: Rules, laws, and guidelines established by governments or regulatory bodies to govern and oversee activities within the cryptocurrency industry. Regulatory efforts aim to ensure consumer protection, prevent fraud, and maintain market integrity.

9. Security Flaws: Vulnerabilities or weaknesses in the code or infrastructure of a cryptocurrency project that can be

exploited by malicious actors to compromise the security and functionality of the project.

10. Smart Contracts: Self-executing contracts with the terms of the agreement between buyer and seller being directly written into lines of code. Smart contracts automatically execute and enforce contract terms when predefined conditions are met.

11. Transparency: A characteristic of blockchain technology and cryptocurrency projects that allows participants to verify transactions and project details in a public and auditable manner.

12. Due Diligence: Thorough research and investigation conducted by investors or participants before engaging with a cryptocurrency project. Due diligence aims to assess the project's legitimacy, viability, and potential risks.

13. Resilience: The ability of the cryptocurrency ecosystem to withstand and recover from adverse events, such as fraud, market crashes, or security breaches, while maintaining its core functions.

14. Privacy: The ability of participants in the crypto ecosystem to conduct transactions and engage in activities without revealing personal or transactional information to the public.

15. Innovation: The creation and implementation of new ideas, technologies, or approaches that enhance the functionality, security, and utility of cryptocurrencies and blockchain technology.

16. Global Collaboration: Cooperative efforts among participants, regulatory bodies, and organizations from different parts of the world to create consistent standards, share best practices, and address challenges within the cryptocurrency industry.

17. Trustless Systems: Cryptocurrency networks and applications designed to function without requiring trust in centralized intermediaries, as transactions and processes are verified and executed through cryptography and consensus mechanisms.

18. Financial Inclusion: The practice of making financial services and opportunities accessible to underserved and unbanked populations around the world through decentralized technologies and cryptocurrencies.

Supplementary Materials

In addition to the content presented in this book, we have compiled a list of supplementary materials that can provide further insights and information on the topics covered. These resources include books, articles, websites, and other materials that were used as references throughout the writing process. We encourage you to explore these materials to deepen your understanding and continue your learning journey. Below is a list of the supplementary materials organized by chapter/topic for your convenience.

Introduction:

Nakamoto, S. (2008). Bitcoin: A Peer-to-Peer Electronic Cash System. Retrieved from https://bitcoin.org/bitcoin.pdf

Chapter 1: The First Altcoins:

Lee, C. M. (2011). Litecoin: An Innovative and Secure Cryptocurrency. Retrieved from https://litecoin.org/docs/litecoin-paper.pdf

Tapscott, D., & Tapscott, A. (2016). Blockchain revolution: how the technology behind bitcoin is changing money, business, and the world. Penguin.

Chapter 2: Decentralized Finance Experiments:

Mougayar, W. (2016). The Business Blockchain: Promise, Practice, and Application of the Next Internet Technology. Wiley.

Hoskinson, C., & Wood, G. (2015). Ethereum: A secure decentralized generalised transaction ledger. Ethereum Project Yellow Paper, 151.

Chapter 3: The Great ICO Gold Rush:

Engel, D. (2017). Initial Coin Offerings: Financing growth with cryptocurrency token sales. Tabb Group.

Howey, S. (1946). SECURITIES EXCHANGE ACT OF 1934, Release No. 33-2106. Retrieved from https://www.sec.gov/litigation/admin/33-2106.htm

Chapter 4: Hacking and Exploits:

Tapscott, D., & Tapscott, A. (2016). Blockchain revolution: how the technology behind bitcoin is changing money, business, and the world. Penguin.

Swan, M. (2015). Blockchain: Blueprint for a new economy. O'Reilly Media, Inc.

Chapter 5: Social Engineering and Manipulation:

Mitnick, K. D. (2002). The art of deception: Controlling the human element of security. John Wiley & Sons.

Cialdini, R. B. (2007). Influence: The psychology of persuasion. HarperCollins.

Chapter 6: Learning from Mistakes:

Narayanan, A., Bonneau, J., Felten, E., Miller, A., & Goldfeder, S. (2016). Bitcoin and Cryptocurrency

Technologies: A Comprehensive Introduction. Princeton University Press.

Antonopoulos, A. M. (2014). Mastering Bitcoin: Unlocking Digital Cryptocurrencies. O'Reilly Media, Inc.

Chapter 7: Regulation on the Horizon:

G20, Financial Stability Board. (2019). "Crypto-Assets Work" Regulatory Approaches to Crypto-Assets. Retrieved from https://www.fsb.org/2019/07/crypto-assets-work-regulatory-approaches-to-crypto-assets/

U.S. Securities and Exchange Commission (SEC). (2021). Statement on "Framework for 'Investment Contract' Analysis of Digital Assets." Retrieved from https://www.sec.gov/news/public-statement/digital-asset-securites-issuuance-and-trading

Conclusion:

Tapscott, D., & Tapscott, A. (2016). Blockchain revolution: how the technology behind bitcoin is changing money, business, and the world. Penguin.

Mougayar, W. (2016). The Business Blockchain: Promise, Practice, and Application of the Next Internet Technology. Wiley.

www.ingramcontent.com/pod-product-compliance
Lightning Source LLC
LaVergne TN
LVHW012112070526
838202LV00056B/5702